Secret Stories of Mickey Mouse

Untold Tales of Walt's Mouse

Jim Korkis

Theme Park Press
The Happiest Books on Earth
www.ThemeParkPress.com

© 2018 Jim Korkis

No part of this publication may be reproduced, distributed, or transmitted in any form or by any means, including photocopying, recording, or other electronic or mechanical methods, without the prior written permission of the publisher, except for brief quotations embodied in critical reviews and certain other non-commercial uses permitted by copyright law.

Although every precaution has been taken to verify the accuracy of the information contained herein, no responsibility is assumed for any errors or omissions, and no liability is assumed for damages that may result from the use of this information.

Theme Park Press is not associated with the Walt Disney Company.

The views expressed in this book are those of the author and do not necessarily reflect the views of Theme Park Press.

Theme Park Press publishes its books in a variety of print and electronic formats. Some content that appears in one format may not appear in another.

Editor: Bob McLain
Layout: Artisanal Text

ISBN 978-1-68390-162-4
Printed in the United States of America

Theme Park Press | www.ThemeParkPress.com
Address queries to bob@themeparkpress.com

Dedicated to David Gerstein who for decades has preserved and shared the history of Mickey Mouse and in so doing has enriched Disney history for all of us.

Contents

Introduction xi

How Was Mickey Mouse Created? 3

Foreign Names of Mickey Mouse 5

Mickey Cartoons: Mickey and the Oscar 7

Talking Mickey: Celebrities 8

Where Does Mickey Live? 10

Mickey Cartoons:
Three Mickey Cartoons Disney Banned 12

Mickey Music: What? No Mickey Mouse? 14

Talking Mickey: Walt on Mickey's Birth 15

Mickey Easter Eggs 19

Mickey Imposter: 'Air Pirates' 21

Mickey Cartoons:
Why Isn't It Called 'Steamboat Mickey'? 23

Mickey Mouse As A Derogatory Term 25

Mickey Imposter: Evil Mickey Attacks Japan 27

Little Mouse on the Prairie 29

The Magic of Mickey's Circles 31

Husband Possessed by Mickey Mouse 32

Mickey Imposter: Milton Mouse 33

How Tall Is Mickey? 35

Talking Mickey: Animator Ward Kimball 37

Mickey Cartoons:
The Horrifying Mickey Cartoon 39

Mickey Cartoons:
Mickey's Two Benefits for Orphans 40

The Charlotte Clark Mickey Mouse Doll 41

Mickey's 50th Birthday 43

Peg Leg Pete's Ever Changing Peg Leg 45

Mickey Mouse NOT Named After Mickey Rooney 47

Floral Mickey 49

Mickey Mouse Rides Never Built 50

Talking Mickey: More Celebrities 51

First Mickey Mouse Cartoon: Plane Crazy 53

When Is Mickey Mouse's Birthday? 56

Mickey Comics:
Birth of the Mickey Mouse Comic Strip 58

Adolf Hitler Loved Mickey Mouse 60

Mickey Mouse Stamps 61

Men Behind the Mouse: Roy Williams 62

Mickey Cartoons:
The Only Three Fab Five Cartoons 63

Mickey's (W)alter Ego 64

Mickey Imposter: Moscow Mickey 66

'Mickey Mouse Theater of the Air' 68

'Mickey Mouse Theater of the Air Episode' Guide 70

Mickey Comics:
The Speechless Mickey Comic Strip 72

Mickey Music: 'Minnie's Yoo Hoo' 73

Hollywood Mickey 76

Mickey Saves Depression Businesses 78

Mickey Comics: Uncensored Mouse 80

Why Does Mickey's Tail Sometimes Disappear? 82

Talking Mickey: Animators on Mickey Mouse 84

Mickey Comics: Mickey Attempts Suicide 86

Mickey Imposter: Mickey in Vietnam 88

Voting for Mickey Mouse 90

Where Do the Stories Come From?
'Traffic Troubles' (1931) 91

Are Mickey and Minnie Married? 92

The Mickey Mouse Club Creed 94

The Mouse That Ate Public Domain 95

Mickey Cartoons:
Ten Mickey Cartoons Never Made 96

Talking Mickey: Walt on Mickey's Personality 98

Men Behind the Mouse: Ub Iwerks 100

The First Mickey Mouse Ride 102

Keeps on Ticking 103

Mickey Military Insignia 104

Mickey Comics: DeMolay Mickey 105

Mickey Cartoons: 'The Plight of the Bumblebee' 106

Mickey's Nephews: Morty and Ferdie 108

The Disney Channel's
New Mickey Mouse Cartoons 109

Why Does Mickey Wear
White Gloves and Big Shoes? 111

Where Do the Stories Come From?
'Mickey's Kangaroo' (1935) 112

Who Does Mickey Mouse's Voice? 113

Mickey's Voice: Walt Disney 115

Mickey's Voice: Jimmy MacDonald 117

Mickey's Voice: Wayne Allwine 119

Mickey Imposter: Filthy Mickey 121

Talking Mickey: Walt on the Mickey Audience 123

Jungle Mickey 125

Mickey Mouse 1935 127

Why Did Mickey Mouse's Eyes Change? 129

Where Do the Stories Come From?
'The Castaway' (1931) 131

Mickey's First Books 132

Men Behind the Mouse: Fred Moore 134

Mickey Imposter: Count Cutelli 136

Mickey Cartoons: Hollywood Party 138

Minnie Moments 140

Talking Mickey: Walt on Mickey's Appearance 141

Hidden Mickey 143

Hidden Mickeys You May Have Missed 145

Fantasmic! 147

Mickey Cartoons: The Talking Dog 149

Mickey at Sea 151

Mickey Cartoons: From Mouse to Duck 153

Mickey Mouse Ears 155

'Partners' Statue 157

Mickey's Girlfriend: Minnie Mouse 159

Men Behind the Mouse: Floyd Gottfredson 162

Mickey Mouse Kills King Kong 164

Mickey Balloons 166

Mickey Mouse Revue 167

Mickey Mouse Costumed
Training Instructions (1973) 169

Brief History of Costumed
Theme Park Character 171

Men Behind the Mouse: Paul Castle 174

Ear Force One 176

Mickey Imposter: Mickey at 60 178

LiMOUSEine 180

Mickey on 'The Mickey Mouse Club' (1955-1958) 182

Mickey Cartoons: First Mickey Mouse
Animated TV Commercials 184

Mickey Loves a Parade 186

Mickey Moments 187

Mickey Cartoons: 'Sorcerer Mickey' 188

A Dozen Appearances of Sorcerer Mickey 190

Men Behind the Mouse: Paul Murry 192

The Chaplin Mouse 194

The University of the Air
(NBC Radio Broadcast Fall 1948) 196

Acknowledgements 199
About the Author 201
More Books from Theme Park Press 203

Introduction

I love Mickey Mouse. He is loyal, brave, compassionate, funny, optimistic, adventurous, and so much more.

I still have my well worn *How to Draw Mickey Mouse* booklet that I got as a kid at the Art Corner at Disneyland. I still wear my vintage Mickey Mouse wristwatch that was the only inheritance I was bequeathed by my late uncle decades ago who had worn it proudly for years. I can't remember any time of my life where Mickey was not a part of it in some way, either through comics, cartoons, or the parks.

Mickey Mouse will celebrate his 90th birthday on November 18, 2018, and yet he remains timeless. Mickey Mouse is a unique pop-culture phenomenon embraced by audiences of all ages around the world. While he physically resembles a three-foot-tall black mouse, spiritually he is a clever and appealing young boy. He was created by Walt Disney in 1928.

Mickey's instantaneous popularity was due to a number of factors: the artistic skill of Ub Iwerks, the storytelling ability of Walt Disney, the novelty of sound on film, and the perfect timing of appearing as a scrappy "everyman" whose indomitable spirit and good humor overcame challenges at the beginning of the Great Depression.

In addition to being a popular animated cartoon star, Mickey is a significant presence in everything from comics to video games to theme parks to toys to food items to just about anything else imaginable.

The Disney company officially described Mickey Mouse for the copyright infringement case Walt Disney Company v. Transatlantic Video Inc., U.S.D.C., Central District of Ca., Case No. CV-91-0429 (1991) in the following way:

Disney's copyrighted character Mickey Mouse is perhaps the most universally known and loved cartoon character in the world. For generations, children and adults alike have been entertained by Mickey Mouse, who has appeared in hundreds of Disney animated motion pictures, television shows, video cassettes, comics, books, and in various other media. Indeed, the Mickey Mouse character identifies and symbolizes Disney itself.

Mickey Mouse shared the same philosophy of life as Walt Disney and transitioned at the same time from a rural background into a more sophisticated Hollywood environment. Walt was the original voice for the character and was the acknowledged "keeper of the Mouse" when it came to decisions about his creation.

Mickey is more than merely a corporate icon, more than a costumed character at theme parks, and more than just another well-known cartoon personality. He is uniquely ingrained in the DNA of several generations of fans all around the world. He transcends time and is forever young and a symbol of optimism that everything will turn out all right in the end.

In the following pages you'll find a lighthearted but informative chronicle of Mickey Mouse including rarely told, never told, and previously mis-told stories in self-contained chapters to celebrate the Happiest Mouse on Earth.

Why? Because we like you!

Jim Korkis
Disney Historian
July 2018

Secret Stories of Mickey Mouse

How Was Mickey Mouse Created?

Walt Disney went to his film distributor, Charles Mintz, in New York to ask for more money to produce the second series of Oswald the Lucky Rabbit cartoons. Mintz offered less money. He had set up his own animation studio and had secretly hired Walt's staff. Walt did not own the character.

Walt and his wife boarded the train back to Los Angeles on March 13, 1928.

Walt told interviewer Tony Thomas in 1959:

> So I had to get a new character. And I was coming back after this meeting in New York, and Mrs. Disney was with me, and it was on the train—in those days, you know, it was three days over, three days from New York. ... Well, I'd fooled around a lot with little mice, and they were always cute characters, and they hadn't been overdone in the picture field. They'd been used but never featured. So, well, I decided it would be a mouse. ... Well, that's how it came about. ... I had [his name as] "Mortimer" first and my wife shook her head, and then I tried "Mickey" and she nodded the other way and that was it.

Roy E. Disney, Walt's nephew, said:

> [The train story] has been told so many times that you don't know what's true. The name part I'm sure of. I often heard my father and Walt say, "Thank God we didn't name him Mortimer!"

Walt's wife, Lillian told Don Eddy in the August 1955 issue of *The American* magazine:

> [Walt] was a raging lion on the train coming home. ...All he could say, over and over, was that he'd never work for anyone again as long as he lived. He'd be his own boss. ... I was in a state of shock, scared to death. He read the script [for *Plane Crazy*] to me, but I couldn't focus on it.

I was too upset. The only thing that got through to me was that horrible name, Mortimer.

Horrible for a mouse, at least. [Lillian actually told Walt it was a "sissy" name.] When I blew up, Walt calmed down. After a while, he asked quietly, "What would you think of Mickey? Mickey Mouse?" I said it sounded better than "Mortimer" and that's how Mickey was born.

There had been plenty of mice in the Alice Comedies and even the Oswald the Rabbit cartoons. While Walt may have thought of a mouse character and a possible storyline on that train trip, it is more likely that once he arrived in Los Angeles he spent time with his brother, his wife, and animator Ub Iwerks coming up with the character.

Essentially, Mickey was a "mouse-ified" version of Oswald the Rabbit (originally designed by Iwerks) with mouse ears replacing rabbit ears and a mouse tail replacing the small rabbit tail. Even the shorts remained the same.

Iwerks said:

Pear-shaped body, ball on top, couple of thin legs. You gave it long ears and it was a rabbit. Short ears, it was a cat. Ears hanging down, a dog. ... With an elongated nose, it became a mouse.

Iwerks later told his sons who asked if he had any resentment that he didn't get enough credit for designing Mickey Mouse, "It was what Walt *did* with Mickey that was important, not who created him."

Disney animator Frank Thomas, one of Walt's fabled Nine Old Men, put it this way:

Ub Iwerks was responsible for the drawing of Mickey, but it was Walt Disney who supplied the soul. The way Mickey reacted to his predicaments, how he tried to extricate himself from a situation he could not control, never giving up and eventually finding a solution. That was all Walt.

Foreign Names of Mickey Mouse

Mickey Mouse is perhaps the most universally known and beloved personality in the entire world.

Animator Ward Kimball said:

> Four years after he first appeared, Mickey was a household word whether the house was in China, Moscow, or Beverly Hills. Whether people were watching in Hong Kong, Paris, or Cairo, they didn't need to follow any dialog. They could simply laugh at what was happening on the screen. You can't imagine how popular he was everywhere and with everyone.

Just like any other famous film actor, Mickey Mouse's name remains the same in many other languages. Keeping the same name is also important for international trademark purposes, but in some countries, Mickey Mouse's name is sometimes translated in fanciful but recognizable ways:

- Afrikaans: Mickie
- Bulgarian: Miki Maus
- Chinese: Mi Lao Shu (Mandarin)
- Chinese: Mai Kay Shiu Shu (Cantonese)
- Esperanto: Micjo Muso
- Estonian: Mikki Hiir
- Finnish: Mikki Hiiri
- German: Micky Maus
- Greek: Mikki Maous/Miky Maoye
- Hungarian: Miki Eger
- Icelandic: Mikki Mus
- Indonesian: Miki Tikus

- Italian: Topolino ("Little Mouse")
- Japanese: Mickey Ma-u-su
- Latin: Michael Muulus
- Lithuanian: Peliukas Mikis
- Malaysian: Miki Tikus
- Norwegian: Mikke Mus
- Polish: Miki
- Portuguese: Rato Mickey
- Rumanian: Miki Maus
- Russian: Mikki Maus
- Serbo-Croatian: Ujka Miki
- Spanish: El Raton Miguelito
- Slovenian: Miki Miška
- Russian: Mikki Maus
- Swedish: Musse Pigg
- Turkish: Miki
- Vietnamese: Mick-Kay
- Yugsoslavian: Miki Maus

Mickey Cartoons: Mickey and The Oscar

Ten of Mickey Mouse's theatrical cartoon shorts were nominated for an Academy Award:

- *Mickey's Orphans* (1931)
- *Building a Building* (1933)
- *Brave Little Tailor* (1938)
- *The Pointer* (1939)
- *Lend A Paw* (1941)
- *Squatter's Rights* (1946)
- *Mickey and the Seal* (1948)
- *Mickey's Christmas Carol* (1983)
- *Runaway Brain* (1995)
- *Get a Horse!* (2013)

The only Mickey cartoon to win an Oscar was *Lend A Paw*, a Technicolor remake of the earlier black-and-white Mickey cartoon *Mickey's Pal Pluto* (1933) about Pluto saving a kitten from drowning and then getting jealous of Mickey's attention to the little ball of fur.

Walt Disney was given a special Oscar for the creation of Mickey Mouse in 1932. Some press reports claimed that the award signified the "first non-human to win an Oscar" even though the Oscar was for Walt, not Mickey. It was only the second time a special Oscar was presented. The first was given to Charlie Chaplin who was scheduled to present the award to Walt but missed the ceremony entirely.

Mickey has presented Oscars in the Animated Short Subject category three times (1978, 1988, 2003) and each appearance was tied to one of his birthday celebrations (50th, 60th, 75th).

Talking Mickey: Celebrities

ACTRESS JULIE ANDREWS: "I am always filled with joy at how readily Mickey is embraced. We need more like him in this world."

ACTOR DICK VAN DYKE: "Mickey was my first introduction to humor and comedy. Mickey's character was always visually funny to me. He was the good guy."

MAGICIAN DAVID COPPERFIELD: "Mickey is magical. He looks great from every angle. He's proof that an idea can be so pure, so specific, yet universal that it can transcend every barrier and last forever."

ACTOR FESS PARKER: "When I was in grade school, my most prized possesion was a yellow slicker with Mickey's picture on it."

AUTHOR IRVING WALLACE: "Mickey is just one of those guys who never gets older. He is a miracle. He is of a special planet where we never grow old, or achy, a perfect place without politicians and poverty—that is the world of Mickey Mouse."

FORMER U.S. PRESIDENT JIMMY CARTER: "Mickey Mouse has been beloved by three generations of Carters. Bringing smiles to the faces of children of all nationalities, he is an ambassador of goodwill and a peacemaker who speaks the universal language of friendship."

FORMER U.S. PRESIDENT GERALD FORD: "In the summer of 1964, I took our two oldest sons to visit Disneyland. We met Mickey Mouse. We were struck by his great, childlike presence and how he embodied so much of Walt's wise, playful spirit."

ASTRONAUNT BUZZ ALDRIN: "Mickey transcends being just a character. He's a symbol of the magnitude of the entire Disney dynasty."

TALK-SHOW HOST LARRY KING: "When Mickey Mouse waves at you in a parade or on the screen, you almost *have* to smile. When Mickey is around, somehow things seem a little brighter."

FILM-MAKER GEORGE LUCAS: "The appeal of Mickey will continue forever, because if he hasn't reached a saturation point by now, he never will. Everyone just loves him."

PLAYWRIGHT ARTHUR MILLER: "Mickey is 'Everyman.' He is honest, decent, a good sportsman. He is little David who slays Goliath."

ACTRESS HAYLEY MILLS: "Mickey Mouse was part of my childhood and he is part of my children's childhood. He's a wonderful link to your past and to the future. He's an experience we all share."

SYNDICATED COLUMNIST BOB GREENE: "Mickey Mouse is the quintessential symbol of innocence. Subliminally, he represents a lot of things we've lost. He represents how things used to be simple and fun and free of darkness."

FORMER U.S. PRESIDENT BARACK OBAMA: "It's always nice to meet a world leader who has bigger ears than me."

ENTERTAINER BOB HOPE: "And to think it all started with a gentle mouse...Boy, they don't build mice the way they used to! I hope I look as good as he does when I reach his age. Mickey, thanks for the memories."

Where Does Mickey Live?

Officially, according to the Disney company, Mickey Mouse lives in Mouseton (a variation on the name of the city of "Houston") near Duckburg.

In the earliest animated cartoons, Mickey lived in a rural area with farms, wide-open spaces, rustic devices, and barnyards filled with a variety of animals. In the early Mickey Mouse comic strips drawn by Floyd Gottfredson, Mickey's hometown was called Silo Center although this name was never used in the animated cartoons.

In 1939, Gottfredson used the name "Mouseville" as the name for the more urban city where Mickey lived and worked. He used it again in several Mickey Mouse comic-strip stories in the 1950s. Disney Publishing used that name in comics it produced for the foreign markets in the 1960s through the 1980s.

To the general public, it was assumed that Mickey Mouse either lived in Burbank, California (the home of the Disney studio), or Hollywood (the home of the movie stars). *Mr. Mouse Takes a Trip* (1940) had Mickey leaving for his trip from the Burbank train station. *Mickey's Kangaroo* (1935) had Mickey receiving a crate addressed simply to "Mickey Mouse Hollywood."

When Mickey fills out his official tax form on the cover on the March 14, 1942, issue of *Liberty* magazine, he lists his address as "Hollywood, California." *American Magazine*, in March 1931, wrote that "Mickey Mouse receives great stacks of fan mail. Some of the letters are just addressed to 'Mickey Mouse-Hollywood.'"

With the opening of Disneyland in 1955, it was stated that Mickey lived in his own clubhouse at the park that was planned to be installed on Tom Sawyer Island.

In 1988, with the opening of Mickey's Birthdayland at the Magic Kingdom in Florida, Mickey and Minnie's houses were on the outskirts of Duckburg, home of Donald Duck and his relatives.

With the release of *Who Framed Roger Rabbit* in 1989 and the opening of Mickey's Toontown at Disneyland in 1993, it was established that Mickey lived in Toontown. In 1990, starting with the stories in the Disney comic books, the Disney company established that Mickey lived in Mouseton and that is his official residence today.

The name for the town was going to be "Mouseville," but at the time on Saturday morning television there was a cartoon series produced by animator Ralph Bakshi with Mighty Mouse living in Mouseville. To avoid confusion, a new name that was uniquely Disney owned was created.

The name for the town was going to be "Mouseville" as had been established decades earlier by cartoonist Floyd Gottfredson but had fallen into disuse. At the same time on Saturday morning television there was a popular cartoon series produced by animator Ralph Bakshi with the character of Mighty Mouse also living in a city called Mouseville.

To avoid any possible confusion, it was decided that a new name should be created that was uniquely Disney owned. Either writer Michael T. Gilbert or one of the comic book editors, David Seidman or David Cody Weiss, came up with the name "Mouseton."

Mickey Cartoons: Three Mickey Cartoons Disney Banned

Between 1930 and 1950, animation studios produced thousands of cartoons containing racial stereotypes. These cartoons were a product of their times where cultural sensitivities were much different. Like radio shows, movies, comic strips, and stage shows that relied on these same exaggerated stereotypes for humor, they were intended to be funny and not hurtful.

While the Disney studio was the lightest offender, it still produced some cartoons with these references. In particular, instances were common where an explosion or soot from a chimney would temporarily make a character look like he was wearing the infamous black-face makeup associated with the old minstrel shows as a sight gag.

In *Mickey Steps Out* (1931), at the end of the cartoon, Pluto is covered with soot and smiles to the audience and says, "Mammy!" This sequence has been cut from all recent airings along with similar scenes in other cartoons.

However, a few Mickey cartoons had their entire premise revolve around a racial stereotype situation. When the Disney Channel came on the air in 1983, these cartoons were reviewed and banned from airing:

Trader Mickey (1932). When Mickey and his boatload of musical instruments are captured by cannibals, he cleverly teaches the natives how to play them rather than cooking him and Pluto. This film was to be a spoof of the popular 1931 MGM film *Trader Horn*. Pinto Colvig does his "Goofy" voice for the Cannibal chief. The caricatured black cannibals, a conceit used in just about all cartoons featuring similar characters, made this offensive.

Mickey's Mellerdrammer (1933). Mickey and the gang perform their own low-budget melodrama based on Harriet Beecher Stowe's 1852 novel *Uncle Tom's Cabin* in a barn converted to a theater. Mickey and the gang are in black-face to tell the familiar story in a comedic fashion. Mickey performs both as Uncle Tom and as Topsy. Mickey sticks a firecracker in his mouth, lights it, and when it explodes the ashes paint his face black.

Mickey's Man Friday (1935). Mickey is shipwrecked on an island of cannibals but rescues one from being eaten whom he names "Friday" just like in the Daniel Defoe 1719 novel *Robinson Crusoe*. Together they build a booby-trapped stockade to hold off an attack by the tribe and eventually escape the island. Billy Bletcher who voices Pete in the Mickey cartoons does the voice of "Friday," a highly comedic character but unfortunately sometimes reminiscent of a jungle monkey.

Mickey Music: What? No Mickey Mouse?

A Gardner Rea cartoon in the March 20, 1931, issue of *LIFE* magazine showed a group of wealthy, sophisticated socialites walking out of a movie theater upset and despondent. The caption underneath read: "No Mickey Mouse!"

The phrase "What? No Mickey Mouse?" was popular in the early 1930s from those with Depression-era paychecks feeling they were getting shortchanged to see a movie without a Mickey Mouse cartoon as part of the program.

That occurrence was referenced in the Warner Bros. live-action film *Lady Killer* (1933) where actor James Cagney played theater usher Dan Quigley:

> Slug, a movie patron [*entering the movie theater*]: Hey, you got a Mickey Mouse on the bill today?
>
> Dan Quigley: No, not today.
>
> Slug [*disappointed*]: What? No Mickey Mouse?
>
> Dan: No, no Mickey Mouse.
>
> Slug: Why?
>
> Dan: Because he's makin' a personal appearance in Jersey City.
>
> Slug: Oh, you're trying to kid somebody, heh?
>
> Other patron: Come on, Slug, let's get our dough back.

England's King George V refused to go to the movies unless a Mickey Mouse cartoon was shown. His wife, Queen Mary, came late to tea rather than miss the end of a charity showing of the cartoon *Mickey's Nightmare* (1932).

Eleanor Roosevelt, wife of former U.S. president Franklin D. Roosevelt said, "My husband always loved Mickey Mouse and he always had to have a Mickey Mouse animated short playing in the White House on movie nights."

Irving Caesar (1895–1996) is perhaps best known as the lyricist of "Tea for Two," "Swanee," "Just A Gigolo," "Ten Cents a Dance," and "Animal Crackers in My Soup." Caesar wrote and published over 700 songs in his lifetime.

Caesar created a novelty song called "What! No Mickey Mouse? (What Kind of a Party Is This?)" during the 1932 election urging listeners to vote for Mickey. It was not widely recorded, but it became a hit for veteran bandleader and popular radio personality Ben Bernie and his band. Bernie himself did the vocal in a "talk/sing" manner with "all the lads" in the band doing the backup chorus. Even Bernie's version does not always stick to these original lyrics:

> When Noah planned his famous ark, he knew just what to do
> He searched until he found a park and walked off with the zoo.
> With lions, tigers, monkeys, donkeys he sailed the ocean wide
> And when he lined them up on deck, 'twas then some coo-coo cried,
> What? No Mickey Mouse? What kind of a party is this?
> Your lions roar, your tigers snore, I've heard them roar and snore before.
> I don't see why you make a fuss about the hippopotamus.
> Your dogs bow wow, your cats meow.
> I know that you can milk a cow
> But Mickey makes me laugh and how and I want Mickey now.
> So where's that tricky mouse?
> That slicky, wacki, wicki, bolsheviki Mickey Mouse?
> Vote for Mickey Mouse!
> And make him our next president!"
> To Congress he is sure to say, "Meow, meow. Okay. Okay.
> Ja. Ja. Yes. Yes. Si. Si. Oui. Oui.
> How dry I am; have one on me.
> And then he'll cry, "Give me the facts.
> Give me my axe; I'll cut your tax!"
> He'll show us all what can be done when he's in Washington!
> So, let's give Hoover's house
> To tricky, wacki, wicki, bolsheviki Mickey Mouse.

The use of the word "tricky" was meant to rhyme with "Mickey" and was also done in previous songs like "Mickey Mouse" fox trot by Harry Carlton in 1930 and "Mickey Mouse (We All Love You)" from 1931.

The sheet music for Caesar's song was spotlighted in the 1932 United Artists marketing catalogs to theaters. United Artists was distributing Mickey Mouse cartoons. The cover featured a pie-eyed Mickey Mouse strumming a one-string homemade guitar (a standard image done by animator Les Clark for merchandise use) and the phrase "Published by License Arrangement with Walt Disney" but no Disney copyright.

Musician and comedic actor Phil Harris sang a cover version of the song on a 45-rpm record single with "Minnie's Yoo Hoo" on the reverse side in 1970. The record was perhaps in conjunction with Harris' voice work in the Disney animated feature *The Aristocats* released that same year. It was released as Vista Record Label #477.

Harris substituted the phrase "Nixon's House" for "Hoover's House" on the recording. Herbert Hoover had been U.S. president when the song was originally written, but in 1970 Richard Nixon now held the office of president. Some earlier versions of the song simply substituted the words "the White House" for "Hoover's house."

The left library in the Walt Disney World Twilight Zone Tower of Terror attraction has a trumpet on a bookcase referencing an episode from that popular television series. Underneath it is the sheet music for "What! No Mickey Mouse? (What Kind of a Party Is This?)" which must have still been popular when lightning struck the hotel in 1939 and sent it to another dimension of both time and space.

Talking Mickey: Walt On Mickey's Birth

"It seems like yesterday that Mickey Mouse first romped across our drawing board. He was born of a desire to move ahead in this great entertainment industry. He symbolized for us the breaking of a chain with the past and the beginning of a new career.

"I got the idea, I suppose, when I was working in an office in Kansas City. The girls used to put their lunches in wire waste baskets and everyday the mice would scamper around in them after crumbs. I got interested and began collecting a family in an old box. They became very tame and by the time I was ready to turn them loose, they were so friendly, they just sat there on the floor looking at me.

"Yes, I had [a pet mouse] during my grade school days in Kansas City. He was a gentle little field mouse. I kept him in my pocket on a string leash. Whenever things seemed to get a bit dull between classes, I would let him roam about on his leash under the seats to get laughs from the other kids. And he got laughs until the teacher rather sharply disagreed with my sense of extracurricular activities and made me keep the little beastie home.

"Perhaps it was the fond memory of him—and of others of his clan who used to pick up lunch crumbs in our first cartoon studio, the family garage—that came to mind when we needed so desperately to find a new character to survive. Mickey Mouse's country forefathers, you might say.

"In Kansas City, I kept one mouse in an overturned wire waste basket and eventually trained it by hitting him on the nose with the eraser on the end of my pencil to stay inside a large circle I drew on a sheet of paper at the top of my drawing board. He was my pet. While I worked, he would comb his whiskers and lick his chops and I fed him little bits of cheese.

"When I decided to go to California, I took him to a vacant lot in the best neighborhood I could find to release him. That mouse that had played on the drawing board didn't seem to want to go. He stood around looking at me. I had to stamp my foot on the pavement and yell at him to make him beat it. That's the last I ever saw of him.

"Mickey Mouse, to me, is the symbol of independence. He was a means to an end. He popped out of my mind onto a drawing pad on a train ride from Manhattan to Hollywood at a time when the business fortunes of my brother Roy and myself were at lowest ebb and disaster seemed right around the corner. Because of his popularity, we were able to go on and attempt the things that were to make animation a real art.

"So I was all alone and had nothing. Mrs. Disney and I were coming back from New York on the train and I had to have something—I can't tell them I've lost Oswald—so, I had this mouse in the back of my head, because a mouse is sort of a sympathetic character in spite of the fact that everybody's a bit frightened of a mouse—including myself."

Mickey Easter Eggs

An Easter egg is a hidden feature or image on a video, video game, or computer program that can only be accessed by following secret instructions. The term comes from the tradition of finding hidden eggs on Easter Sunday.

Walt Disney Treasures: Mickey Mouse in Black and White (Volume One)

From Disc 1's bonus features menu, highlight Mickey's cowboy hat and press Enter for a newsreel about the original Mickey Mouse Club in Worchester, Massachusetts, from the 1930s, and the sing-along short *Minnie's Yoo Hoo*.

Walt Disney Treasures: Mickey Mouse in Living Color (Volume One)

On Disc 1's main menu, select Mickey's head and press Enter to view a two-and-a-half minute excerpt from Walt's very first television anthology episode, 1954's *The Disneyland Story* where Walt gives the famous "it was all started by a mouse" speech.

In Disc 2's main menu, press Up to highlight the "O" in the word "Mickey Mouse" at the top of the screen. Pressing Enter plays the short *Mickey's Surprise Party*. This five-minute unedited commercial was made in Technicolor for the National Biscuit Company (Nabisco) to show at their 1939 World's Fair pavilions in New York and San Francisco.

Minnie bakes cookies to impress Mickey, but an accident in the kitchen with popcorn ruins them. Mickey and Pluto save the day by rushing to the store and purchasing a variety of Nabisco cookies including Milk Bones for the dogs. In the VHS release *The Spirit of Mickey,* all the Nabisco packaging was replaced by generic products, and all of Minnie's lines referencing the names of the products overdubbed by Russi Taylor.

Walt Disney Treasures: Mickey Mouse in Living Color, (Volume Two)

In Disc 1's main menu, move down to highlight the cane underneath Mickey and Pluto. Press Enter for an eleven-and-a-half-minute black-and-white film clip of Walt Disney and Billy Bletcher recording lines of dialog for Mickey Mouse and Pete, respectively, for the animated short *Mr. Mouse Takes a Trip* (1940).

In Disc 1's bonus features menu, press Down until a musical note becomes highlighted on the right-hand side. Press Enter to see a 1939 promo film Walt Disney made for Standard Oil which includes a brief history of the Disney studio and a Technicolor short featuring Disney characters on parade to support Standard Oil.

Mickey Imposter: 'Air Pirates'

Dan O'Neill is the most infamous of the underground comix artists to use the Disney characters. He did so in his daily *Odd Bodkins* syndicated newspaper strip without arousing the attention of the Disney organization. However, when O'Neill brought together a group of talented underground artists and produced the first issue of the underground comix book *Air Pirates Funnies* in July 1971, Disney took notice.

Disney characters including Mickey, Minnie, Goofy, and Donald were featured in explicit sex and drug activities. The comix book was purposely designed to evoke a remembrance of the DELL comic books of the 1940s that featured Disney characters. O'Neill dubbed his version "HELL Comics." Two issues of *Air Pirates Funnies* and one issue of *Tortoise and Hare* (featuring some of the material planned for the third issue) were produced before Disney finally managed to stop the young artists.

It was O'Neill's first contention that the Disney characters in these "earlier designed versions" reminiscent of Floyd Gottfredson's work from the 1930s were in public domain since they had been unused for years and did not reflect the current Disney versions of the characters. Disney probably found that contention that they had abandoned their rights even more offensive than the images of Mickey and Minnie having sex. Later, O'Neill shifted his defense to claim he was only doing parody.

The US District Court of Northern California granted an injunction against *Air Pirates* in June 1972 and three years later in August 1975 found that "*AIR PIRATES FUNNIES* constituted copyright infringement, trademark infringement, unfair competition and trade disparagement." The matter was appealed to the Ninth District Court of Appeal which in September 1978 reversed the lower court ruling on trademark, competition, and trade disparagement, but upheld the ruling that *Air Pirates Funnies* infringed Disney's copyright.

The attorneys appealed to the US Supreme Court which on January 1979 decided to let stand the lower court rulings, including the $190,000 in damages for copyright infringement that had been assessed by Judge Albert Wollenberg.

The Disney company had spent approximately two million dollars in legal fees as O'Neill continued to ignore the judgment of the courts to cease and desist. He established the MLF (Mouse Liberation Front) and distributed small publications with the classic Disney characters at conventions and art shows.

The Spring 1979 issue of *The Co-Evolution Quarterly* (#21) featured a four-page comic book style story by O'Neill starring Mickey and Minnie Mouse entitled "Communique#1 from MLF" (Mouse Liberation Front). Several previous MLF communiques had been circulated at various comic book conventions. Artists were assigned numbers so that their names did not appear in print.

Disney asked the court to hold O'Neill in contempt along with magazine publisher Stewart Brand and prosecute both of them criminally.

By now, O'Neill was more a nuisance than a threat, especially since the court's decision could be used on future offenders of the Disney sanctity and any other challenges to the earliest character designs so an exhausted Disney legal team eventually decided on a different course of action.

An out-of-court settlement was reached in 1980 stipulating that none of the participants could reveal the terms (common in Disney out-of-court settlements). O'Neill felt that not going to jail constituted a victory for him.

Mickey Cartoons: Why Isn't It Called 'Steamboat Mickey'?

Audiences had never heard of "Mickey Mouse," so naming the cartoon "Steamboat Mickey" instead of *Steamboat Willie* would have had zero box-office recognition and would not have increased attendance.

More importantly, Walt would insist that when an audience went to see a Mickey Mouse cartoon they were seeing the life of Mickey Mouse himself unlike other characters like Bugs Bunny or Woody Woodpecker.

Mickey was merely an actor performing a role just as Clark Gable or Cary Grant would do. The role might have similarities to the actor's personality, but it was indeed a role. This conceit was one of the things that positioned Mickey Mouse in the marketplace differently than other animated characters of the time.

Mickey was not Steamboat Willie; he was portraying the role of a character named Steamboat Willie. In his next film, he might be portraying a different character, even if all of the characters had much of Mickey's own personality.

Most articles refer to the cartoon as a parody of comedian Buster Keaton's last independent silent comedy, *Steamboat Bill Jr.* (1928), which had been released in May 1928 and was very popular.

However, other than the fact that both films feature a steamboat and that Keaton's character is named "Willie" as a diminutive version of "Bill," the cartoon makes no direct references to Keaton's film—unlike Mickey's *Gallopin' Gaucho* (1928), which parodies some of the action and style of the Douglas Fairbanks' silent action film, *The Gaucho* (1927).

While Walt may have hoped that audiences would associate the title with the popular Keaton classic, no direct parody was ever intended. It was just Walt's way of drawing attention to his cartoon.

In the cartoon, the opening music was a popular 1911 song entitled "Steamboat Bill," which also inspired the title—and again, the hope of audience familiarity.

While Walt and many others assumed the song was in the public domain and could be used freely, it was, in fact, still under copyright at the time. Retroactively, Columbia Pictures , the distributors of all the Mickey Mouse cartoons beginning in 1930, had to pay a licensing settlement fee in April 1931 for the use of the music.

In addition, audiences were aware of two other things: the well-known Broadway musical *Showboat*, which premiered in 1927, and the tragic Mississippi River flood of 1927, which led to vast improvements in flood control. As a result, Mississippi steamboats loomed large in the mind of the general public.

Mickey Mouse as Derogatory Term

How did the name "Mickey Mouse" come to represent something substandard, amateurish, trivial, poor quality, irrelevant, senseless, or worthless?

Mickey Mouse and his early cartoons were of the highest possible quality. In fact, his name was used by composer Cole Porter in the 1934 song *You're the Top* to indicate the character's extremely high status.

However, in the early 1940s, some musicians were critical of the close synchronization of the music with the cartoon action where the music literally punctuates every physical motion for comedic effect in a Disney cartoon.

That same type of music was used in circus bands, burlesque, and similar venues, and was considered not "real" music. The term was also used by some musicians for just corny or bland music of any kind that was evident in the Mickey Mouse cartoons.

Early in 1933, Ingersoll-Waterbury of Connecticut began making the first Mickey Mouse watches. Since they were designed for children and had to be made quickly and inexpensively, they got the reputation of being not as well made as a regular watch. By June 1935, over 2.5 million watches had been sold, inspiring poorly produced counterfeits that easily fell apart.

Peanuts cartoonist Charles Schulz wrote:

> I did want a Mickey Mouse watch [in the 1930s] in the worst way. In those days, it cost $2.95 and I saved up my money for one. My mother took me to the local jewelry store to buy one. She asked them if they were really good watches and the guy say that they were okay for what they were, but for a dollar more, I could have a really good watch. So I never did get my Mickey Mouse watch.

Children who grew up with those original watches that often quickly fell apart and had heard dance bands demeaned as "just a Mickey Mouse band" used the phrase "Mickey Mouse" as a term of derision for things and procedures during World War II that had little value.

The use of Mickey as a prejorative has remained to this day with one of the most frequent descriptions of something being unprofessional as a "Mickey Mouse organization."

In the movie *The Godfather Part II*, Fredo's justification for betraying his brother Michael was complaining, "Let Fredo take care of some Mickey Mouse nightclub somewhere!" In the movie *Demolition Man* (1993), Sylvester Stallone's character deals with malfunctioning brakes by yelling, "Brake now, you Mickey Mouse piece of shit!"

Mickey Imposter: Evil Mickey Attacks Japan

Today, the Japanese adore all things Disney, but during the dark days of World War II, Mickey was seen as an icon representing everything evil about a captialistic United States threatening Japan.

It was not just the United States that produced animated cartoons for propaganda purposes. In 1934, Japan released the eight-minute *Omochabako series dai san wa: Ehon senkya-hyakusanja-rokunen (Toybox Series 3: Picture Book 1936)* by Komatsuzawa Hajime. On the internet, it can be found under the title *Evil Mickey Attacks Japan*.

A Japanese island is populated by cute animals and children who sing and dance. One of the animals even resembles a counterfeit Felix the Cat.

However, their happiness is short-lived because from the air they are attacked by an army of Mickey Mouses, riding horrific bat-like creatures who also have Mickey Mouse heads. These villains are assisted by snapping crocodiles and vicious snakes who act like machine guns.

One of the frightened inhabitants appeals to a huge storybook to summon their folk heroes to protect them. Momotaro ("Peach Boy"), Kintaro ("Golden Boy"), Issunboshi ("One-Inch Boy"), and Benkei, a warrior monk, all answer the call to battle the evil Mickey Mouses. The message was that the classic Japanese folklore characters were much more powerful than this recent cultural upstart.

The film was made in 1934 but was dated 1936 supposedly to coincide with the expiration of a naval treaty between the United States and Japan which would eventually lead to the attack on Pearl Harbor.

Through magic, Mickey is defeated and even turned into a decrepit character who hobbles away to a flood of laughter while the residents return to their joyful lives.

Things changed significantly after World War II when many classic Mickey Mouse tin toys were made in Japan and decades later the first foreign Disney theme park, Tokyo Disneyland, was built.

Emperor Hirohito of Japan was a huge fan of Mickey Mouse. He was given a Mickey Mouse watch as a gift during his special tour of Disneyland in 1975. For years, even on formal occasions, he was observed wearing the watch.

In 1979, there was panic when the watch stopped ticking, and a concerned palace chamberlain rushed it to Tokyo experts specializing in American timepieces. Fortunately, the watch merely required a new battery. When Hirohito died in 1989, he was buried at his request wearing his Mickey Mouse watch.

Little Mouse on the Prairie

Mickey Mouse's 60th birthday in 1988 was celebrated by the publication of a special magazine, the opening of Mickey's Birthdayland in the Magic Kingdom in Florida, a television special, *Earforce One* (a hot air balloon in the shape of Mickey's head) touring the United States, and other events, including a flood of commemorative merchandise featuring a new birthday logo.

One of the unique tributes was a 520-acre cornfield in Sheffield, Iowa, planted in the shape of Mickey Mouse's head facing sideways.

Disney Creative Marketing executive Jack Lindquist was flying across Texas one day and realized that he could see circles created by natural gas fields at 35,000 feet. He realized circles could be used to create a Mickey Mouse head silhouette over the most-traveled air route at the time with passengers flying from New York to San Francisco or from Houston to Minneapolis.

He determined that a green cornfield would provide the best color contrast to see Mickey, and consulted Iowa State University agricultural experts for guidance.

The land between Sheffield (population 1,224) and Dougherty was farmed by the Pitzenberger family and the planting was done in secrecy in April. A mile perimeter around the site was taped off. The grand reveal took place August 6–7, 1988, with a parade, music, fireworks, and other entertainment that brought an estimated 15,000 guests. A costumed Mickey Mouse, Minnie, Donald, and Goofy left Disneyland to travel to Sheffield for the party, and *Earforce One* floated overhead.

The event was not solely planned by Disney. In 1988, the towns of Chapin, Dougherty, Messervey, Rockwell, Sheffield, Swaledale, and Thornton joined together to form the Area Community Commonwealth (ACC), which planned the Disney event. The ACC has since dissolved.

Using a design developed with the help of a surveyor and a Disney art director, Joe Pitzenberger with his three sons planted 6.5 million corn plants in the shape of Mickey's head surrounded by 300 acres of oats in a day and a half. It was 1.1 miles from the tip of Mickey's nose to the end of his ear. They harvested 35,000 bushels of corn in October.

Rain eluded other areas of the state that was suffering a drought that summer, but it magically rained on the Mickey crop circle. The event was covered by national major media and overflying airlines for several months alerted passengers to the hidden Mickey down below like a historic landmark.

The Magic of Mickey's Circles

Imagineer John Hench said in a 1975 interview:

> Concerning Mickey Mouse in particular, he triggers something in my mind that refers back to this matter of survival patterns. He is made out of a series of circles. He is not a static thing but very dynamic in the way the circles fall together.
>
> He has been accepted all over the world and there is obviously no problem of people responding to this set of circles. I'm going to oversimplify this, but circles never cause anybody trouble. We have bad experiences with sharp points, with angles, but circles are thing we have fun with—babies, women's behinds, breasts.
>
> Mickey is a series of round shapes that have a distinctive relationship characterized by the flow of one curve into another, creating lines that relate to each other. The size of Mickey's head relative to his face is similar to the proportions of a human baby's head and face. Adult humans have an instinctual nurturing response to creatures with baby-like proportions and features.
>
> So Mickey has made his way while a contemporary known as Felix the Cat didn't get anywhere. He had points all over him, like a cactus. He has practically disappeared, while we couldn't get rid of Mickey if we tried.

Husband Possessed by Mickey Mouse

From the *Orlando Sentinel*, February 24, 1989, about an incident that took place in New York:

> A woman who killed her husband by repeatedly running over him with a car—and who claimed she thought he'd been possessed by Mickey Mouse—has been sentenced to five to fifteen years in prison.
>
> Roseann Greco, 52, of West Islip, was charged with second-degree murder for killing her husband, Felix, in their driveway in 1985. She insisted at the time that the cartoon character had taken over her husband's body.
>
> Mrs. Greco was found mentally competent to stand trial and was convicted of first-degree manslaughter. She could have faced a maximum of eight to twenty-five years in prison.
>
> But Sulfolk County Judge John Vaughn sentenced her Wednesday to the minimum, five to fifteen years. Assistant District Attorney Georgia Tscheimber urged the judge to impose the maximum sentence, arguing that Mrs. Greco posed a threat to her family if released from prison or a mental hospital.
>
> Defense attorney Edward McGuinness said the crime was the result of his client's refusal to take prescribed medication for mental problems. Relatives had asked for the minimum sentence and promised Greco would be "watched carefully and made to keep taking her medication" when released.

Mickey Imposter: Milton Mouse

With the popularity of Mickey Mouse, animation studios began to produce their own cartoons with characters that looked like Walt's mouse including three shorts at Warner Bros. in 1931 featuring "Foxy" from former Disney animator Rudy Ising. The character and his girlfriend had fox ears and tails but looked exactly like Mickey and Minnie.

The three 1931 shorts were *Lady, Play Your Mandolin* (August), *Smile, Darn Ya, Smile!* (September) and *One More Time* (October). The voice performers were not credited and all three shorts eventually fell into public domain.

Ising stated before his death in 1992 that he stopped using Foxy because Walt Disney personally phoned him up and asked him to retire the character because he felt it was too close for comfort in appearance to Mickey.

However, the voice tracks were recorded and animation was already in process for two more 1931 Foxy cartoons: *You Don't Know What You're Doin'* and *Hittin' the Trail for Hallelujah Land*. Ising came up with another character named Piggy who still had some physical similarities to Mickey but with several significant differences like a snout and curly tail and used him in those two cartoons instead.

Foxy and his girlfriend made an appearance after being redesigned to look less like Mickey and Minnie in the September 1992 episode entitled "Two-Tone Town" of the *Tiny Toons* syndicated television show. Even after Ising left Warners, he retained the rights to Foxy.

One of he more blatant attempts were Milton and Rita (earlier referred to as "Mary") Mouse produced by Van Beuren for their Aesop's Fables series. The pair also appeared in three cartoons: *Circus Capers* (1930), *Hot Tamale* (1930), and *The Office Boy* (1930).

On March 31, 1931, Disney sued Van Beuren. Amedee J. Van Beuren on April 3, 1931, issued this statement:

> The only information we have thus far received that such action is pending is contained in articles in the papers. In my judgment the action is entirely without merit or foundation. Aesop's Fables created the characters Milton and Mary Mouse at the inception of the company in 1921 and the company has been using them.
>
> If there has been any imitation, it would appear to be at the door of Walt Disney Productions, whose characters of Mickey Mouse and Minnie Mouse are so similar to ours. As soon as we are served with papers we shall be prepared to defend the action.

Van Beuren forgot to mention that the characters had been recently and radically redesigned by his artists John Foster, Harry Bailey, and Manny Davis to closely resemble Mickey and Minnie.

Disney got a temporary court injunction against Van Beuren on April 30, 1931, from federal judge Cosgrave and a formal decree was issued four months later prohibiting Van Beuren from "employing or using or displaying the pictorial representation of 'Mickey Mouse' or any variation thereof so nearly similar as to be calculated to be mistaken for or confused with said pictorial representation of 'Mickey Mouse.'"

Disney did not ask for any money, even though the original suit clearly stated that "the petitioner demands an accounting, damages and surrender of all profits made on the alleged imitations."

In an interview in the 1960s, Roy O. Disney remembered:

> We just stopped him. That's all we were out to do. We didn't ask any damages. We even let him finish marketing his pictures. We wanted to establish our right. That's what we were after. To establish a copyright like that is a big thing and that's an important thing to do.

How Tall Is Mickey?

In the animated cartoons, Mickey is about three feet tall. In the Disney theme parks, he is about five feet tall. Actually, animation model sheets indicate Mickey is "three heads high" meaning that whatever the size of his head, his remaining body height is twice the size of it. Over the years Mickey has sometimes been drawn to be almost four feet tall.

In the July 1930 edition of the *Standard Casting Directory for Talking Pictures and Stage* that included almost three hundred pages of headshots, contact information, brief résumés, and other information about working Hollywood actors looking for more work, there was a half page devoted to Mickey Mouse.

His agent was listed as "Walt Disney" at the Hyperion Studio in Los Angeles. In addition, Mickey is described as being "two feet three inches tall and weighs eighteen pounds." Later entries had his weight listed as 23 pounds.

In *When The Cat's Away* (1929) and *The Barnyard Battle* (1929), Mickey is about the size of a real mouse.

Walt Disney, in the January 1964 issue of *LOOK* magazine, said:

> And it wasn't well received. It's because we thought of him as a mouse. Then I went back and thought of him as I originally did [as a young boy] and we went on from there. He was a little fellow is what he actually was, a little fellow.

In a 1956 interview, artist Ub Iwerks said:

> I don't recall any special meetings or discussions on how Mickey should look. ... We decided to make Mickey the size of a little boy. We couldn't have him mouse-sized because of scale proportions (in terms of being seen clearly on the screen with objects). We asked ourselves, "What are people going to think?" The size must have been right—people accepted him as a symbolic character,

and though he looked like a mouse he was accepted as dashing and heroic.

Animator Ward Kimball said:

In the old days of cartooning, the characters didn't have much relationship to reality. You could put almost anything into animation and the public accepted it. But whoever heard of a four-foot-tall mouse? That was the problem. Donald Duck, Goofy, Pluto, Clarabelle Cow, and all the rest were drawn to scale. They were believable because they were of a relative size. Then along comes a mouse as big as they are and it stopped working.

Talking Mickey: Animator Ward Kimball

"Mickey was a great character in the early days when the plots were very, very simple. Most of Mickey's antics were based on playing musical instruments or tap dancing or doing something like the Charleston with Minnie. Our dilemma became one of trying to find new, logical material for Mickey, more sophisticated material, if you will.

"Writing for Mickey became very difficult. Mickey began to be relegated to roles that were Boy Scout-ish in nature. And then we just couldn't fit him into anything— so we finally discarded him. Mickey just faded away.

"I've heard people say something to the effect that 'Walt Disney couldn't even draw Mickey Mouse!' I can't imagine where they got such information. Many of Walt's friends and associates will tell you that he not only could but, on hundreds of occasions, did draw Mickey. Mickey Mouse was untouchable. If you made any changes you really had to clear them with 'City Hall' (Walt Disney himself), as they say.

"Drawing Mickey consistently was to use a circle the size of a silver dollar for the close-up shots, a fifty-cent piece for medium close-ups, a quarter for medium shots, a nickel for medium long-shots, and a dime for long shots. The head and fanny sections were made with the same size circle and connected with two lines.

"Something's happened to the Mouse through the middle years. You know, he started out without shoes or gloves. Then he got red pants. His face got rounder. They added eyebrows, and now, most youngsters know him as a cute youngster with a bowtie of all things. He's become a sissy!

"Mickey was really an abstraction. He wasn't based on anything that was remotely real. That's what killed him.

He was the one character in our cast that was not believable. Because when you saw Donald Duck, you accepted him as a duck. He walked like a duck. He was two feet high. Pluto was a real dog. Goofy you accepted as a man. He might have had those ears, but he was a man.

"But what are you going to do with a mouse that's three feet high, where his ears just float. They don't turn in perspective. [He] has this funny black and white division [on his face], has garden hose legs...and this is what happened to Mickey. He finally just became a symbol because he's three feet high and he's a mouse."

Mickey Cartoons: The Horrifying Mickey Cartoon

Live-action films with mad scientists performing horrific experiments were popular in the 1930s, so it was not surprising that Walt Disney decided to parody the format. *Mad Doctor* (1933) features a mad scientist planning a horrible experiment for Pluto. Fortunately, it turns out not to be real, just Mickey's nightmare.

The first black-and-white Mickey Mouse cel set-up ever offered for sale was in 1988 and purchased by Oscar-winning film director Steven Spielberg for $63,800. It is from *Mad Doctor* with Mickey at the top of the stairs with his back toward the audience and skeletons starting to pop up out of the tops of the stairs.

The overlay was not from the film, though the background was original. Mickey and the skeletons were on a cel created in 1934, in black and white as an illustration for page 59 of the David McKay book *Mickey Mouse's Movie Stories Book 2*.

The British Board of Film Censors deemed the cartoon completely unacceptable, not because of scenes of Mickey almost being cut in half or the proposed operation on Pluto's brain, but because of the presence of skeletons, classified as representing the "living dead," one of the forbidden items on the censor list.

Mickey Cartoons: Mickey's Two Benefits for Orphans

In the summer of 1939, with Mickey's birthday coming up again, Walt was going to produce a two-reel short film that theaters could use that fall for the celebration entitled *Mickey's Revival Party*.

Disney characters would arrive at a theater to watch scenes from some of their classic cartoons. Unfortunately, these films were mostly in black and white and the characters had changed their appearance somewhat drastically over the years.

Walt decided that it might be a good idea to just redo several of the old shorts in color. A soundtrack existed. The layout and staging existed. In addition, it might serve as a good training ground for new, inexperienced animators who would have a definite guideline to follow.

So, *Orphan's Benefit* (1934) was redone as *Orphans' Benefit* (1941). The next film scheduled to be redone would have been *Mickey's Man Friday* (1935) followed by *On Ice* (1935) to revise the look of Donald Duck.

While the remake of *Mickey's Man Friday* was in production, the program was cancelled. Walt discovered that remaking the black-and-white cartoons in color was not as inexpensive as he had hoped and also that he found himself anxious to explore new cartoons rather than revisiting the past.

The Charlotte Clark Mickey Mouse Doll

In January 1930, Carolyn "Charlotte" Clark had an idea of how to use her sewing talents to make some money during the Great Depression. She sent her fourteen-year-old nephew, Bob Clampett, who would later become a Warner Bros, cartoon director and creator of *Beany and Cecil*, to the Alex Theater in Glendale, California.

The young teen sat through three consecutive showings in order to see a Mickey Mouse short several times so he could sketch Mickey Mouse. From those sketches, Clark made the first stuffed Mickey Mouse doll. Clampett's father advised her to get Walt Disney's permission before she started making and selling them.

He drove her to the Disney studio. Both Walt and Roy loved the doll. They rented a house near their Hyperion studio that was later nicknamed the "Doll House" for Clark to work on making the doll in three different sizes. Originally, the dolls were purchased by Walt and Roy to give to friends, business acquaintances, and special visitors to the studio.

These dolls often included a personalized embroidered label that read: "A Charlotte Clark creation made especially for Walt Disney, copyright W.D.Productions." The dolls were notable for Clark's renowned sewing craftsmanship that featured a cotton fabric face with felt sculptured shapes, black floss embroidery mouth and face expressions, applied oil cloth pie-cut eyes, tiny buttons, miniature corduroy clothes, cotton- felt hands, feet or shoes, silk-satin embellishments, and hand sewn seams.

She later expanded and did other Disney characters including Minnie, Donald, and Pluto as well as prototype creations for characters that were never mass-produced like the Gremlins from Disney's unmade animated feature and Jose Carioca and Panchito from *The Three Caballeros*.

However, she is best remembered for her first Mickey Mouse dolls that set the high standard by which all future cartoon character dolls would be measured.

After a photo of Walt with one of the dolls appeared in *Screen Play Secrets* magazine in 1930 and several newspapers, the demand for owning one of the figures by the general public became overwhelming.

By November 1930, Clark was producing three to four hundred dolls a week to be sold at two large Los Angeles area department stores, May Company and Bullock's, for five dollars each. The department stores only paid two dollars and fifty cents per doll, and so made an amazing profit. Clark had to employ six full-time seamstresses to meet this goal. Yet the demand continued to exceed what the overworked staff could make.

Some families could not afford the price of the doll in those hard times and Walt felt that every child who wanted a Mickey Mouse doll should have the opportunity to have one.

The McCall Company of New York released Printed Pattern No. 91 in early 1932 based on the Clark design with twenty seven pieces, one transfer, and one tissue sheet of directions at a cost of thirty-five cents so that homemade Mickey dolls could be produced.

Printed across the bottom of the pattern envelope are the specifications that "[t]his pattern sold for individual use only and not to be used for manufacturing purposes." The McCall Pattern No. 91 was available from 1932 through 1939, resulting in thousands of treasured and now highly collectible Mickey and Minnie dolls in the Clark style.

In 1934, Knickerbocker Toy Company in New York started mass-producing Mickey and Minnie dolls based on Clark's patterns. Clark designed their various Disney dolls until 1958. She died December 31, 1960, at the age of 76.

Mickey's 50th Birthday

Mickey's 50th birthday was a year-long celebration in 1978 and generated not only an official "Happy Birthday, Mickey" logo but a variety of commemorative merchandise. This was the first official celebration of Mickey's birthday as being on November 18.

There were retrospective screenings of Mickey's cartoons at several venues, from the New York Metropolitan Museum of Modern Art to the American Film Institute to the Chicago Film Festival.

Animator Ward Kimball accompanied a Disneyland costumed character Mickey Mickey on a special Amtrak train for a 57-city tour. The tour ended at the Broadway Theater (formerly the Colony Theater, where *Steamboat Willie* debuted). A plaque designating the theater as the official birthplace of Mickey Mouse was installed.

Traveling on the same mode of transportation on which he was supposedly created, Mickey made stops in Kansas City, Missouri (the home of Walt's first cartoon studio and where little field mice that Walt befriended lived in the studio and may have inspired the creation of Mickey), Chicago, Illinois (Walt's birthplace), and the White House (where eleven-year-old Amy Carter, the daughter of President Jimmy Carter, welcomed him).

After his appearance at the Broadway Theater in New York (where he met the Broadway cast of the musical *The Wiz*), Mickey and Kimball returned to Los Angeles via Washington, D.C., where he was honored at the Library of Congress.

Kimball recalled the Mickey Mouse Birthday Express train tour:

> The time of day that we stopped at a town didn't matter a bit. Even at two or three o'clock in the morning, there were hundreds of people out there holding their kids up high just to get a glimpse of Mickey as he stepped from

the train or waved to them from the platform of the observation car. I have never gotten over that and realized then the power that Mickey Mouse has as a symbol.

Sometimes the press of people was so great, even after [the costumed] Mickey had gone inside, that it was impossible to move the train out of the station without the danger of hurting someone. I devised a method that solved that problem in most places.

We had cartons of little yellow pin-back buttons that said 'Happy Birthday, Mickey" on them and I would stand on the rear platform and toss those buttons far to the rear of the train. As the people scrambled to pick up the buttons, the train was able to slowly pull out of the station.

Seven huge scrapbooks in the Walt Disney Archives are filled with newspaper clippings from the year-long event. In addition, Mickey received his star on the Hollywood Walk of Fame, making him the first cartoon character to ever receive that honor. People were singing a specially written song, "The Whole World Wants to Wish You Happy Birthday, Mickey Mouse."

A parade was held in his honor at both Disneyland and Walt Disney World during that year.

Mickey's 50th (November 19, 1978), a special episode on *The Wonderful World of Disney* weekly television show, featured celebrities like Johnny Carson and Jonathan Winters honoring Walt's mouse.

Peg-Leg Pete's Ever-Changing Peg Leg

Peg-Leg Pete is the oldest recurring Disney animated character. He originally bullied Alice in the Alice Comedies starting in 1925 as "Bootleg Pete" (referencing not only his leg but his illegal bootlegging activities) and later Oswald the Lucky Rabbit before becoming Mickey Mouse's chief nemesis beginning in *Steamboat Willie* (1928).

Animator Frank Thomas said in 1993:

> For an adversary, we had a surly strongman with a cigar (usually) and a wooden leg, probably to suggest a pirate symbol who audiences would associate with someone who was rough and mean.
>
> The animators could never seem to remember whether the wooden leg was on the right or the left, and in some pictures, even drew him with two good legs but still called him Peg-Leg Pete. However, the biggest problem with the peg leg was doing a walk cycle because he would have to swing the leg around and it messed with the timing.
>
> So we got rid of the peg leg not for socially conscious reasons but because it made things easier for us to animate.

In the animated short *Two Gun Mickey* (1934), Mickey is a cowboy hero who rescues Minnie Mouse from Pete and his gang of outlaws.

Pete switches which leg his pegleg is on several times during the few minutes of this cartoon. One of the most noticeable instances is his jumping on the log bridge with the peg on one leg and when he gets off on the other end, the peg has shifted to the other leg.

In his earliest comic strip appearances Pete's peg leg also proved to be a problem. At first, he sported a knee-high peg leg which was later reduced to an ankle-high prosthesis.

In *Mickey Mouse in Race to Death Valley* (1930) newspaper serial, cartoonist Floyd Gottfredson started the strip drawing the peg leg on Pete's right leg but by the time the story had finished, the peg leg was on the left leg. In the 1941 Mickey comic strip serial *The Mystery of Hidden River*, Pete tells Mickey he now wears a more realistic prosthetic.

Officially, Pete lost his peg leg in the animated shorts after appearing in *Mickey's Service Station* (1935). His name was changed to Black Pete and then just Pete. The peg leg would later pop up again in *Mickey, Donald, and Goofy: The Three Musketeers* (2004) and has occasionally returned in some of his other appearances in different media.

Mickey Mouse NOT Named After Mickey Rooney

Walt Disney originally intended to call his creation "Mortimer Mouse," but at the urging of his wife, Lillian, the name was changed to "Mickey." There is much independent documentation that confirms the story.

Still, actor Mickey Rooney loved telling this anecdote that first appeared in his 1991 autobiography *Life Is Too Short*.

On a lunch break while filming the Mickey McGuire comedies, five-year-old Rooney walked by an open shabby office at Larry Darmour Productions, poked his head in, and introduced himself.

"'Who are you?' I asked the guy working there.

'My name is Walt Disney,' he said. 'Come over and sit on my knee.'

"So I went over and sat on his knee, and there was a mouse he had drawn.

'My gosh, that's a good-looking mouse, Mr. Disney.'

'It sure is, Mickey,' he said, and he stopped and looked into space for a minute. 'Mickey, Mickey,' he said. 'Tell me something, how would you like me to name this mouse after you?'

And I said, 'I sure would like that, but right now I got to go and get a cheese sandwich.' And I jumped down."

Rooney only began telling this fabrication of a story decades after Walt Disney died and there were multiple variations he told, from Walt calling him into an office at Warner Bros. to it being a tuna sandwich.

Mickey Mouse was created in 1928. Mickey Rooney didn't even become Mickey Rooney until he officially changed his name in 1932. He was born Joe Yule Jr. on September 23, 1920, and that was his name in 1928 when he was seven years old, not five.

Rooney got his big break in films at the age of six when he was cast as the lead in a series of several dozen comedy two-reelers beginning in 1927 named for "Mickey McGuire," a character from a popular newspaper comic strip known as the *Toonerville Folks* by Fontaine Fox. Disney had his own studio on Hyperion Avenue since 1925 and his cartoons were distributed by Universal. There never was any connection with any other studio or production company.

The popularity of the "Mickey McGuire" character in films, comic strips, and merchandising may have helped make the "Mickey" name seem familiar to Walt and Lillian, but it was not a chance meeting between Mickey Rooney and Walt Disney that gave the world a "Mickey."

Floral Mickey

When Disneyland opened in July 1955, the very first thing that guests saw was the huge, smiling face of Mickey Mouse created in colorful flowers at the entrance of the park.

Horticulturist Bill Evans, who supervised the landscaping at Disneyland and Walt Disney World, said:

> It was the most photographed location at Disneyland. Everybody took a picture standing in front of it. It was Walt's idea. Just like the face on the title card before every [theatrical] Mickey cartoon and audiences would start cheering and applaud.

Evans built a light wooden framework for the outline of the head and individual sections like the eyes, ears, and nose, and then filled it in with thousands of plants.

Depending upon the seasons and what bedding plants and annuals were available, or even at the whim of the landscapers, the colors might change drastically. Today, it takes over 4,500 plants to make Mickey's face. The whole display can take around 7,000 plants

Originally, the face was just called the Mickey Mouse Planter, but in recent years it has been referred to as the Floral Mickey. Evans stated that it was a "parterre," a French term for an ornamental garden that forms a distinctive pattern.

Mickey Mouse Rides Never Built

Over the decades, Mickey Mouse has been featured prominently in several theme park attractions including the Mickey Mouse Revue, Fantasmic!, Mickey's PhilharMagic, and even his own land with his house. In 2019, Mickey and Minnie's Runaway Railway will open in Disney's Hollywood Studios.

Disney animator Ward Kimball proposed two Mickey Mouse themed attractions that never evolved off the drawing board.

In 1976, Kimball designed an attraction called Mickey's Mad House. Using the traditional wild mouse coaster like the one used for the Primeval Whirl at Disney's Animal Kingdom, guests would have careened madly back and forth through this indoor dark ride not being able to see clearly where they were going while experiencing some of the wild antics in early black-and-white Mickey Mouse animated cartoons.

In the early 1980s, when a movie pavilion was planned for Epcot's Future World between the Imagination Pavilion and The Land Pavilion, a version of the Great Movie Ride then called Great Movie Moments would have been included. Kimball came up with an additional dark ride for the pavilion tentatively titled Mickey's Movie Land that would have allowed guests in omnimover vehicles to glimpse a tongue-in-cheek, behind-the-scenes process of making a classic Mickey Mouse cartoon.

Talking Mickey: More Celebrities

ANIMATOR/HISTORIAN JOHN CANEMAKER: "I think of Mickey as an actor, a jolly, cheerful symbol that embodies the American spirit of optimism, can-do energy, and versatility."

PERCUSSIONIST/RECORD PRODUCER DICK SCHORY: "Within a year of his creation, he could do something no other mouse had ever done before. He could talk. People would often sit through a feature twice to see Mickey again. Walt often said, 'There's a lot of the Mouse in me!'"

ACTOR FESS PARKER: "Absolutely amazing it all came from one little cartoon scratched on one little piece of paper… and a great sense of storytelling."

AUTHOR/ILLUSTRATOR MAURICE SENDAK: "Oh, I adored Mickey Mouse when I was a child. He was the emblem of happiness and funniness. You went to the movies then, you saw two movies and a short. When Mickey Mouse came on the screen and there was his big head, my sister said she had to hold onto me. I went berserk."

AUTHOR EDWIN C. HILL: "Perhaps Mickey's celebrity is not so amazing, after all, when one remembers that he came to us at the time the country needed him most—the beginning of the Depression. He has helped us laugh away our troubles, forget our creditors, and keep our chins up."

ARTIST ANDY WARHOL: "Mickey Mouse is my favorite actor! Minnie Mouse is my favorite actress!"

AUTHOR HARLAN ELLISON: "Every man, woman, and child on the planet knows Mickey Mouse, Sherlock Holmes, Tarzan, Robin Hood, and Superman."

AUTHOR JOHN UPDIKE: "Mickey's persistence springs from something timeless in the image that has allowed it to pass in status from a fad to an icon."

SINGER DOLLY PARTON: "I have been in love with Mickey Mouse longer than I have been in love with my husband."

SONGWRITER RICHARD M. SHERMAN: "My dad would run black-and-white short films of Mickey Mouse on the wall of our New York apartment. The images filled the room. Mickey was my best friend. One day, part of the film burned in the projector and it broke my heart. Dad spliced the film and I still watched it over and over."

HUMORIST FRAN LEBOWITZ: "Mickey Mouse has a cuteness that is so American. I have always liked Mickey's hands. I think all rodents should wear gloves."

ENTERTAINER ART LINKLETTER: "Mickey Mouse was the turning point for Walt. That little mouse opened the world for an old country boy."

COMEDIAN ROBIN WILLIAMS: "You try and do special things for your kid. I thought, 'I'll take him to Disneyland. That'll be fun.' Mickey Mouse to a three year old is a six-foot-tall rat! The only reason Mickey has three fingers is because he can't pick up a check."

COMEDIAN DANNY THOMAS: "Mickey, especially, promotes that feeling of comfort. Even in these politically scary times, he gives us hope and joy and relief from the everyday problems we face."

POP ARTIST KEITH HARING: "Mickey Mouse is ultimately a symbol of America more than anything else."

ACTRESS/STATESWOMAN SHIRLEY TEMPLE BLACK: "In the 1930s the Speaker of the House in Finland said, 'We look to America to lead us in our fight for democracy. But unfortunately, the main cultural influences are that little girl [Shirley Temple] and your mouse'."

First Mickey Mouse Cartoon: Plane Crazy

While *Steamboat Willie* is officially considered the first Mickey Mouse cartoon because it was widely shown to the general public, Walt Disney and Ub Iwerks actually produced two other silent black-and-white cartoons featuring Mickey in 1928 that preceded *Steamboat Willie*: *Plane Crazy* and *Gallopin' Gaucho*.

Plane Crazy is a simple story of a rural young boy, portrayed by Mickey Mouse without gloves or shoes, who tried to emulate America's latest hero, aviator Charles Lindbergh, by building and flying his own plane.

In May 1927, "Lucky Lindy" had become a hero with his solo airplane trip in the *Spirit of St. Louis* across the Atlantic from New York to Paris, and Walt hoped to leverage that overwhelming interest in aviation in attracting an audience to his new cartoon character.

The first few installments of the 1930 Mickey Mouse newspaper comic strip written by Walt and illustrated by Ub Iwerks told a similar version of this cartoon short including a panel of Mickey looking at a picture of Lindbergh for inspiration.

Plane Crazy was animated by Iwerks from start to finish. Iwerks was isolated from the rest of the Disney studio where other animators who had signed with distributor Charles Mintz's new studio were finishing up their commitments to produce the final Oswald the Lucky Rabbit cartoons.

Iwerks produced over 8,000 separate drawings by himself for the cartoon, an unheard-of feat. Walt and Iwerks created a 6-page, 36-panel animation story script as a guideline. Iwerks began work the last week of April 1928 and by the second week of May cels were ready to be inked and painted.

Walt put in three benches in his garage at his home on Lyric Avenue for a makeshift studio where Walt and Roy's wives (Lillian and Edna) along with Walt's sister-in-law (Hazel Sewell) inked and painted Iwerks' artwork onto cels.

Mike Marcus was the cameraman and shot the cel artwork at night at the Disney studio after the animators had gone home, with Walt personally cleaning up all traces of the work afterwards so it wouldn't be discovered the next morning by the defecting animators who might tell Mintz.

Plane Crazy was finally previewed at a theater at Sunset and Gardner in Hollywood on May 15, 1928. The title card stated "A Walt Disney Comic—by Ub Iwerks."

Walt had coached the theater pianist on how to accompany the action and slipped him a little extra money as well to punch up the music. Reportedly, the picture got quite a few laughs and applause from the audience that Iwerks remembers being almost a full house.

Walt sent a print of the film to New York to be viewed by distributors but received no offers. The novelty of animation was fading in popularity and, in addition, distributors were intrigued by what impact the recently introduced use of sound on film would have on the industry.

Encouraged by the audience response to the cartoon, Walt and Iwerks began work almost immediately on the second Mickey Mouse cartoon, *Gallopin' Gaucho*, a loose take-off on a popular Douglas Fairbanks silent film, *The Gaucho* (1927).

At least one major movie studio, MGM, saw *Plane Crazy* but made no offer to finance a series. Reportedly, one executive claimed that a three-foot-tall mouse would frighten pregnant women in the theater audience.

Roy O. Disney, in small handwriting, entered into his ledger book the amounts (which included production and prints) for the first three Mickey Mouse cartoons:

PLANE CRAZY: $3,528.50
GALLOPIN' GAUCHO: $4,249.73
STEAMBOAT WILLIE: $4,986.69

When *Steamboat Willie* began to attract attention and it appeared that Mickey Mouse would become the star of a series of cartoons, Walt had Kansas City theater organist Carl Stalling write music scores for both *Plane Crazy* and *Gallopin' Gaucho* so he could release more Mickey Mouse shorts quickly to take advantage of the public's interest.

Plane Crazy was eventually released theatrically March 17, 1929, at the Mark Strand Theater in New York after a new soundtrack had been added in December 1928.

Walt Disney filed for a copyright on "Mickey Mouse in Plane Crazy" on May 26, 1928, as an unpublished work. That copyright was never updated. On August 9, 1930, Walt Disney copyrighted the sound versions of the first two silent films, *Plane Crazy* and *Gallopin' Gaucho*.

The climax of the cartoon is inappropriate for today's audience as it focuses on Mickey Mouse trying to force Minnie to give him a kiss. Mickey even tries to intimidate her with dangerous aeronautical maneuvers in hopes of scaring her to kiss him in order to stop. When he does finally grab Minnie to kiss him, Minnie angrily slaps Mickey in the face to get him to stop and finally has to jump out of the airplane.

When Is Mickey Mouse's Birthday?

Officially, Mickey Mouse's birthday is November 18, 1928. That also makes it the official birthday of Minnie Mouse.

Of the Fab Five, only Mickey, Minnie, and Donald Duck have official birthdays. Pluto and Goofy evolved through several cartoons so it is difficult to credit a particular cartoon with the emergence of those two characters.

Former Disney archivist Dave Smith determined through a program from the Colony Theater in New York that Mickey's first truly public appearance was in *Steamboat Willie* on November 18, 1928, and so, for the 50th celebration in 1978, that became the official birthday.

"The Walt Disney Company is now reaching a point in its history where there are many significant anniversaries to celebrate, and the company has come to realize that these celebrations can be very useful marketing tools," Smith shared with Disney historian Jim Fanning in 1988 about why an official birth date for Mickey Mouse had to be established.

For the previous fifty years, the Disney company selected any date from September through November as Mickey Mouse's birthday primarily as a merchandising tool to encourage theaters to rent Mickey Mouse cartoons and to do special promotions like parties.

For instance, on October 25, 1931, the *Los Angeles Times*, after contacting the Disney studio, affirmed that Mickey Mouse's birthday was October 24 and that was when his third birthday was celebrated.

In *Film Pictorial* magazine dated September 1933, Walt Disney himself is quoted as saying:

Mickey Mouse will be five years old on Sunday. He was born on October 1, 1928. That was the date on which his first picture was started so we have allowed him to claim this day as his birthday.

Mickey's seventh birthday was celebrated on September 28, 1935, and movie theaters were encouraged to book entire programs of Mickey Mouse and Silly Symphony cartoons as part of the celebration. It was called Mickey's Lucky Seventh Birthday.

In 1938, Mickey's birthday was celebrated on September 27. According to an 1968 issue of *Disney News* magazine, Mickey's 40th birthday was to be officially celebrated September 27, 1968.

Mickey's 50th birthday was a year-long celebration in 1978 and generated not only an official "Happy Birthday, Mickey" logo but a variety of commemorative merchandise and special events. This was the first official celebration of Mickey's birthday as being November 18 and it has remained on that date for the last forty years.

Mickey Comics: Birth of the Mickey Mouse Comic Strip

By the start of 1930, Mickey had already appeared in fifteen animated adventures (with nine more scheduled for that year). Inspired by that popularity, January 13, 1930, saw the introduction of the Mickey Mouse comic strip from King Features Syndicate. Those early strips were written by Walt himself up until May 17, 1930.

Walt said:

> [I considered] other ways to exploit characters like the Mouse. The most obvious was a comic strip. A letter came to me from King Features wanting to know if I would be interested in doing a comic strip featuring Mickey Mouse. Naturally, I accepted the offer.

Ub Iwerks had quite literally drawn the first three Mickey Mouse animated cartoons by himself and was the natural choice to transfer Mickey's antics to the newspaper page. Most newspapers headed the strip as "Mickey Mouse by Iwerks" with Walt Disney's famous signature not appearing until March 11, 1930.

The strip began as a gag-a-day type until April 1, 1930, when it went into story continuities at the request of King Features. Just as in the animated cartoons, Mickey got into actual fistfights and sometimes carried a gun as he faced bandits, pirates, wild animals, and a host of other menaces.

In the April 29, 1930, strip, Mickey locates a stack of cheese in the basement of a mansion and Walt has him exclaim, "My gosh! What cheese—if I only had a bottle of beer!!!"

After the eighteenth strip, Iwerks left the Disney studio and his inker, Win Smith, reluctantly continued drawing the gag-a-day format until he was replaced by Floyd Gottfredson.

Gottfredson remembered:

> Walt had continued to write the strip, including the first seven weeks of the first continuity I drew. He had been trying to get Win Smith to do the writing as well as the drawing but for some reason he didn't want to. This was one of the reasons for Smith's leaving the studio.
>
> I took over the drawing with the May 5, 1930, episode and I took over the writing with the May 19, 1930, release. I wrote the daily until late 1932. After that time, the continuities were written by different writers.

Gottfredson ended up working on the strip for over forty-five years until 1975.

In 1938 it was estimated there were 20,400,000 readers of the daily Mickey Mouse comic strip. In the 1990s, the strip was finally discontinued, as were many others, because of declining newspaper readership.

Adolf Hitler Loved Mickey Mouse

In his diary entry for December 22, 1937, Adolf Hitler's propaganda minister Joseph Goebbels wrote:

> I am giving the Fuhrer...18 Mickey Mouse films [as a Christmas gift]. He is very excited about it. He is very happy about these treasures which will hopefully bring him much fun and relaxation.

The reason for this gift was that during July 1937 in Hitler's private screening room, the Führer watched five Mickey Mouse cartoons and laughed loudly.

Yes, this is the same Adolf Hitler that tried unsuccessfully to ban Mickey Mouse in Germany in 1937 because he noticed young Germans (and even some of his own staff) wearing Mickey Mouse pins and emblems rather than a swastika. He tried again with greater success in 1941 to ban Mickey.

In October 1931, a Nazi newspaper printed the following statement after seeing young people decorating themselves with little emblems of Mickey:

> Youth, where is thy pride? Mickey Mouse is the most miserable ideal ever revealed. Mickey Mouse is a plan to promote weakness.
>
> Healthy emotions tell every independent young man and every honorable youth that the dirty and filth-covered vermin, the greatest bacteria carrier in the animal kingdom, cannot be the ideal type of animal. ... Down with Mickey Mouse! Wear the Swastika Cross!

Mickey Mouse Stamps

When a United States commemorative stamp was released in 1968, it featured the smiling face of Walt Disney but not Mickey Mouse. Postal regulations at that time prohibited the placing of a Disney copyright notice on its stamps.

However, other countries around the world did not have similar restrictions, so Mickey first appeared on a ninety lira stamp from the tiny republic of San Marino in 1970 with an appropriate copyright notice.

Multiple foreign countries have issued stamps with Mickey Mouse on them in the hopes that fans and collectors will purchase them and never use them for the intended purpose of mailing something. In that way, the money stays with the government since it never has to provide the service. The U.S. soon realized that this was a money-making idea.

The Art of Disney: Friendship stamp series, issued in 2004 by the United States Postal Service, included Mickey Mouse. These designs were created by Dave Pacheco and Peter Emmerich. The Art of Disney: Celebration stamps in 2005 featured Mickey Mouse with Pluto, and The Art of Disney: Romance stamps in 2006 featured Mickey Mouse with Minnie Mouse. In 2007, The Art of Disney: Magic postage stamps included Sorcerer Apprentice Mickey. In 2008, The Art of Disney: Imagination had Mickey as Steamboat Willie.

Men Behind the Mouse: Roy Williams

Gag man Roy Williams recalled that he was sitting in Walt's office one day when Walt "looked up at me and said, 'Say, you're fat and funny looking. I'm going to put you on [*The Mickey Mouse Club* television show] and call you the Big Mooseketeer.' The next thing I knew I was acting."

"The three-hundred-pound pixie," as he was described, was a story man at the Disney studio who, remembering the gag in *The Karnival Kid* (1929) where Mickey tips his ears to Minnie like a hat, invented what is still the most popular merchandise item at Disney theme parks: the Mickey Mouse ears hat.

Williams was also one of the writers for the Mickey Mouse comic strip and some comic book stories. When he died on November 7, 1976 as a result of a heart attack, he went out in style, as reported by the *Motion Picture Screen Cartoonists Newsletter*:

> Ever a colorful character, Roy stipulated that he, much to the astonishment of [Forest Lawn Hollywood Hills] morticians, but not his many friends, be interred wearing his Mickey Mouse Club hat and his Mickey Mouse Club T-shirt, with his name inscribed on the front thereof, in full regalia. It was so done.

Mickey Cartoons: The Only Three Fab Five Cartoons

During Walt Disney's lifetime, Mickey only appeared with the rest of the entire Fab Five (Minnie Mouse, Donald Duck, Goofy, and Pluto) in three animated cartoons. (The term was inspired by the Beatles' nickname of the Fab Four.)

On Ice (1935). Mickey teaches Minnie to skate. Goofy tries an unusual method of ice fishing. Donald teases Pluto by putting skates on his paws.

Hawaiian Holiday (1937). Mickey and Donald play the slide guitar and ukulele while Minnie dances in a grass skirt. Goofy tries to surf and Pluto battles a starfish. It won the prize for best short subject from the International Film Exhibition in Venice, Italy. This cartoon was made roughly 22 years before Hawaii became a state (August 21, 1959) and was inspired by a holiday trip Walt and his family took to the island paradise where Walt tried to surf.

Pluto's Christmas Tree (1952). Mickey chops down a tree for Christmas not realizing it is the home of Chip'n'Dale and that he accidentally brings them inside his house with the tree. Pluto is continually thwarted in his attempts to show Mickey the truth. The short ends with carolers Goofy, Donald, and Minnie on Mickey's front lawn briefly singing "Deck the Halls."

Mickey's (W)alter Ego

IMAGINEER JOHN HENCH: "Mickey was definitely Walt's alter-ego. Like Mickey, Walt was optimistic—he certainly had enormous faith in himself, and, of course, Mickey has enormous faith in himself—he takes on giants and whatnot. We knew how he'd act under a given circumstance. We knew basically how he'd behave because of Walt."

ROY E. DISNEY, WALT'S NEPHEW: "Mickey really is Walt in a lot of ways. Mickey has all those nice impulses Walt had, the kind of gut-level nice guy he was."

ANIMATOR OLLIE JOHNSTON: "Nobody but Walt could do the Mouse. He was the only guy who felt how to handle Mickey always correctly. After *The Sorcerer's Apprentice*, there really wasn't a good Mickey because Walt wasn't as involved. I never felt that Mickey was part of me, the way other characters I've drawn were. I always felt Walt's presence very strongly when I worked with Mickey. Mickey reflected Walt's boyhood personality and did a lot of things Walt had wanted to do himself—rescuing princesses, beating up bullies, putting on variety shows."

AUTHOR IRVING WALLACE: "Is Mickey a man or a mouse? Though the men who make Mickey always refer to him as the Mouse, it is their policy never to treat him as one. Disney animators think he's a lot like Walt Disney. 'The same soulful eyes,' they say, 'the same beaky face, the same trick of falling into pantomime when at a loss for words.'"

OVERLAND MONTHLY, OCTOBER 1933: "Walt is Mickey. If Mickey is good, it is because Walt is good. Every characteristic of Mickey's, from the lift of his eye-brow to his delightful swagger, is Walt's own. Mickey is not a mouse; he is Walt Disney."

ANIMATOR FRANK THOMAS: "Mickey was Walt, and Walt was Mickey. Mickey reached his height in the days when Walt did the voice. The gag man could put in gags, but Walt was the only one who could say, 'Hey, you're not using this guy right.' He would act out what he was talking about. He got everybody laughing. Ub Iwerks was responsible for the drawing of Mickey, but it was Walt Disney who supplied the soul. The amazing mouse was indeed Walt's alter ego, echoing the personality traits, mores, outlook on life, and dreams of his boss. He acted out Walt's fantasies in a remarkably personal way."

WALT'S WIDOW, THE LATE LILLIAN DISNEY: "Whenever I see Mickey Mouse, I have to cry. Because he reminds me so much of Walt."

Mickey Imposter: Moscow Mickey

In 1988, for Mickey Mouse's 60th birthday, a Disney animation festival sponsored by a Soviet commission on cinematography was kicked off with a gala premiere in Moscow. It was the first time Disney shorts and feature films, except for *Snow White and the Seven Dwarfs* (1937), had officially and legally been viewed in the USSR.

A costumed Mickey Mouse joined a costumed Misha the Bear, the mascot for the 1980 Moscow Olympics, for a tour of Red Square. Interestingly, the Russian children kept a discreet distance from Mickey and just politely waved. However, they swarmed around Misha with much laughter.

Roy E. Disney and other Disney executives visited the famed animation studio, Soyuzmultfilm. A special cartoon was presented to Roy titled *The Marathon*.

A little over two minutes in length, the cartoon shows a young boy in black silhouette going to a line that divides the screen image in half. It is like a mirror with the young boy on one side and the classic black-and-white Mickey Mouse in black silhouette on the other side.

At the top of the screen is the number 1928, the year Mickey debuted. The number clicks to a zero and starts clicking upwards to the number 60. During this time, the young boy ages into a young man and finally an old, overweight man.

During the short, Mickey and the other character have fun dancing and playing until the ravages of age slows down the old man. Mickey whistles to call over a chair for the man to sit on. Another young boy runs up to the man and is directed back to the line where the number clicks back to zero and the assumption is that the same adventure will be repeated again with this new boy and an ageless Mickey.

The short was co-directed by Mikhail Tumelya and Alexander Petrov and was written by Tumelya, who animated on the short as well. The very catching music was by A. Varlahov Lilivokalany. D. Murkis, B. Bresler, Sasha Zuzkevich, and Polene Tumelya were used as dancer reference.

It was produced by I. Boyarsky and A. Zalessky at the School for Advanced Studies for Screen Writers and Directors Beyelorusfilm, with Soyuzmultfilm Studios, in Moscow.

Roy E. Disney said:

> It was an absolutely beautiful tribute to Mickey. We were all choked up. My wife was in tears.

Mickey Mouse Theater of the Air

During the Golden Age of Radio (1920–1950), listeners could tune in the dial on their huge living room radio and hear a wide variety of programming. Walt Disney himself (often doing the voice of Mickey Mouse and sometimes accompanied by Clarence Nash voicing Donald Duck) popped up on several radio shows to promote Disney cartoons.

Looking for additional funds and publicity for the almost completed *Snow White and the Seven Dwarfs* (1937), Walt hesitantly agreed to produce a radio show sponsored by Pepsodent entitled *Mickey Mouse Theater of the Air*.

The premise was that through the use of the Magic Mirror, Mickey and the gang could venture through time and space to meet everyone from Long John Silver to Mother Goose to Robin Hood. They visited Snow White twice as well as Cinderella and Sleeping Beauty.

Walt only did Mickey's voice for the first three weeks. From the fourth show on, the voice of Mickey was comedian Joe Twerp whose previous comedy act relied on being an excitable, stuttering person who confuses words. He had been considered for the role of Doc, a similar personality, in Walt Disney's *Snow White,* but Roy Atwell was chosen to supply the voice instead.

The writers for the show were Bill Demling (who had supplied material for big-name radio comedians like Ed Wynn and Joe E. Brown) and Eddie Holden. In addition, Glanville Heisch, the creator of the popular radio show *Cinnamon Bear,* was on board as a writer and director. His skill at writing verse and songs is evident in the Disney radio program.

Music direction was by Gordon "Felix" Mills, one of radio's most active orchestra leaders of the era who directed thirty-three musicians for the show.

Broadcast from a theater studio on the RKO lot (RKO was releasing the Disney animated films), Minnie Mouse was performed by Thelma Boardman with Stuart Buchanan doing Goofy. Donald Duck was voiced by Clarence Nash and Clara Cluck was Florence Gill.

The announcer was John "Bud" Hiestand who also supplied the voice of the Magic Mirror. The other voices on the show were supplied by popular performers including Billy Bletcher (as Old King Cole and Judge Owl), Hans Conreid (as the Pied Piper), Bea Benaderet (portraying Miriam the Mermaid in the kingdom of King Neptune), Walter Tetley, and even Mel Blanc who did a variety of different voices as he also did on multiple other radio shows.

The show would supposedly air weekly beginning on October 5, 1937, with Mickey Mouse hosting along with a weekly live guest star (actor Leslie Howard on the audition record) but that Donald Duck would mess things up.

Because Walt was so overwhelmed with work on his first feature film, actor J. Donald Wilson was selected to do Mickey's voice. One newspaper reported that it was "the first time anyone other than Walt Disney himself was allowed to speak for Mickey."

Roy Disney flew to New York in September to close the deal, but it fell apart because of a dispute over money.

Walt wrote in a 1938 issue of *Radio Log* magazine:

> I'm letting Mickey and the rest of my gang go on the air, although I've been advised against it. It's a rather logical direction in which we can expand. We expect to develop new ideas and personalities we can use in our pictures. We look upon radio as a new stimulus, a challenge—something which will give us fresh ideas and a better perspective on our work.

Mickey Mouse Theater of the Air Episode Guide

When the contract ended after thirteen weeks, Pepsodent renewed *Mickey Mouse Theater of the Air* for the remaining seven weeks of that season, but then cancelled it.

Critic Aaron Stein of the *New York Post* wrote:
> All the strength, the vigor and logic of the Disney films lies in the pictures. The voices, the music and the sounds are usually funny and effective, but they register only as sound effects which point up the pictures. On the air they offered only disembodied sound effects.

The twenty Theater of the Air episodes were:

- January 2, 1938: *Robin Hood*
- January 9, 1938: *Snow White Day*
- January 16, 1938: *Donald Duck's Band*
- January 23, 1938: *The River Boat*
- January 30, 1938: *Ali Baba*
- February 6, 1938: *South of the Border*
- February 13, 1938: *Mother Goose and Old King Cole*
- February 20, 1938: *The Gypsy Band*
- February 27, 1938: *Cinderella*
- March 6, 1938: *King Neptune*
- March 13, 1938: *The Pied Piper*
- March 20, 1938: *Sleeping Beauty*
- March 27, 1938: *Ancient China* (with a guest appearance by Snow White!)
- April 3, 1938: *Mother Goose and the Old Woman in a Shoe*
- April 10, 1938: *Long John Silver*

- April 17, 1938: *King Arthur*
- April 24, 1938: *Who Killed Cock Robin?*
- May 1, 1938: *Cowboy Show*
- May 8, 1938: *William Tell*
- May 15, 1938: *Old MacDonald*

The final twenty-two page, half-hour episode from May 15, 1938, had Mickey and the gang trying to save Old MacDonald's farm. Old MacDonald was voiced by Cliff Arquette, who may be best remembered today for his character of Charley Weaver. With the help of the Magic Mirror, Mickey and his friends go back thirty years to try to save the farm from foreclosure.

Squire Perkins (voiced by Billy Bletcher) mistakenly believes that Minnie Mouse is the farmer's daughter and offers to exchange the mortgage for her hand in marriage. After he is horrified that the real daughter is Priscilly (voiced by a constantly hiccupping Mel Blanc), he pays MacDonald to tear up the contract and everyone celebrates with apple cider.

Mickey and the gang return to the present and because they have been working so hard during the length of the series the Magic Mirror sends them to Vacation Land to relax.

With the tune "Heigh Ho" playing the background, the announcer says:

> And so with Mickey and the gang headed for Vacation Land we bring to a close the last program in the present series, brought to you by the Pepsodent Company. This program has come to you from the Disney Little Theatre on the RKO lot. The orchestra and musical arrangements were under the direction of Felix Mills. John Hiestand speaking for the Pepsodent Company. This is the National Broadcasting Company.

Mickey Comics: The Speechless Mickey Comic Strip

From September 1, 1958, to March 17, 1962, two different Mickey Mouse newspaper strips were available at the same time. The first Mickey Mouse comic strip that began in 1930 was still appearing in newspapers drawn by Floyd Gottfredson and featured story continuities.

King Features Syndicate felt that perhaps a gag-a-day daily strip done in the pantomime style with no dialog balloons or captions might be easier to sell to foreign countries since there would be no need for the cost of translation and re-lettering.

Writers included Milt Banta, Roy Williams, and Julius Svendsen. Artists included Ken Hultgren, Manuel Gonzales (who had been drawing the regular Sunday Mickey Mouse comic strip), and Riley Thomson.

An oblivious Mickey Mouse walks along and steps into an open manhole. He recovers in the hospital. As he leaves and waves goodbye to a nurse, he is about to step into another open manhole. Another strip had Mickey outside gardening with a hoe when a bird swoops by and steals his hat. Mickey is not angry because in the final panel he sees the bird has placed the hat in the crook of some branches as a makeshift nest.

Despite expectations, few international newspapers chose to purchase this strip and it quietly disappeared after a little over three years.

Mickey Music: "Minnie's Yoo Hoo"

Minnie Mouse's typical greeting in the early Mickey Mouse cartoons was not "hi" or "hello" but a melodic and flirtatious "yoo hoo!"

For Mickey's tenth cartoon, *Mickey's Follies* (1929), the first original song for a Disney short appeared. It lasted about one minute (700 drawings) with music by Carl Stalling and lyrics by Walt Disney. Entitled "Minnie's Yoo Hoo," it became so popular that it became the theme song for the original Mickey Mouse clubs held in local movie theaters. The lyrics reflected the rural barnyard atmosphere of the early Mickey Mouse cartoons.

It was the first Disney song to be released on sheet music and was published by Villa-Moret, which was based in Los Angeles. It is the only Disney sheet music that credits Walt on any Disney song.

A roughly three-minute animated sing-a-long short also called "Minnie's Yoo-Hoo" was produced for club meetings. The reel opens with a short title card introducing Mickey as the master of ceremonies and his Mickey Mouseville Jazz Band.

Re-using animation from *Mickey's Follies* mixed with some new animation like Mickey peering out from behind a curtain, applauding at the end and a different background, this sing-a-long trailer was approximately 400 feet long and was sold by the Disney studio for $16.50 to theaters. Mickey sings the song once and then encourages the audience to sing along a second time with the lyrics on the screen.

An instrumental version of the song was used over the title credits of the Mickey Mouse theatrical cartoons from *Jungle Rhythm* (1929) through *Mickey's Mechanical*

Man (1933), making it Mickey's theme song for the early 1930s.

Melotone released the song as a single (M12028) by Leo Zollo and his Orchestra on January 1931. It was also shown being played on a phonograph in the Mickey Mouse comic strip on October 28,1930.

Around 1968, a "rinky-tink" new version of the song was recorded for *The Mickey Mouse Anniversary Show* (December 1968) directed by Ward Kimball for *The Wonderful World of Color*. This version later appeared as the B side of a 45 novelty single by musician and comedian Phil Harris released in 1970. Kimball also used the same version over the end credits for the syndicated television show *The Mouse Factory* (1972) that he produced and directed.

Kimball remembered:

> [I found a] wild little tune in a 1929 cartoon, *Mickey's Follies*. The song was great. It had a wonderful "antiquey," tinny quality about it. Then I realized that it had been our official Mickey Mouse song in the early thirties. But I couldn't remember the [song's] title.
>
> With a little sleuthing, we learned that Carl Stalling had written it. He still lived near the studio [after a long career providing music for Warner Bros. cartoons] so I called him. He told me, "What do you want with that old thing?" It's called 'Minnie's Yoo Hoo.' I just made it up. Nothing special about it."

There are multiple farm references in the opening verse including the fact that Minnie, like a real mouse, would live in a burrow in the outdoor chicken coop, with the phrase "henhouse steal" referring to sneaking into the area to steal chickens. It is also the first time that Minnie is officially referred to as Mickey's sweetheart, though it has been fairly obvious in the previous cartoons:

> I'm the guy they call little Mickey Mouse
> Got a sweetie down in the chicken house
> Neither fat nor skinny

> She's the horse's whinny
> She's my little Minnie Mouse!
> When it's feedin' time for the animals
> And they howl and growl like the cannibals
> I just turn my heel to the henhouse steal
> And you'll hear me sing this song.

The first chorus again emphasizes the barnyard aspects, in particular the plethora of farm animals. In *Mickey's Follies*, it is Minnie herself who pipes in with a melodic "yoo hoo" at that final point in the song:

> Oh, the old tomcat with his meow, meow, meow!
> Ol' hound dog with his bow-wow-wow!
> The crow's caw-caw!
> And the mule's hee-haw!
> Gosh what a racket like an ol' buzz saw!
> I have listened to the cuckoo "kuke" his coo-coo!
> And I've heard the rooster cock his doodle doo-oo
> With the cows and the chickens
> They all sound like the dickens
> When I hear my little Minnie's "yoo-hoo"!

It was rumored that musician Carl Stalling may have sung the song for the original cartoon in an overly articulated manner. The animation is also overly exaggerated in an attempt to correctly synchronize the words with Mickey's mouth and his movements. Up to this time the Mickey cartoons had successfully synchronized sounds with the actions on the screen, but there had not been any dialog which was a new challenge.

Hollywood Mickey

- "Mickey has a bigger screen following than nine-tenths of the stars in Hollywood," wrote Hearst newspaper gossip columnist Louella Parsons in 1931.

- In 1933, Mickey Mouse received 800,000 pieces of fan mail, more than any other star in Hollywood.

- Mickey Mouse was the first animated character to receive a star on the Hollywood Walk of Fame in November 13, 1978, in honor of his 50th birthday that year. It is located at 6925 Hollywood Boulevard in front of Grauman's Chinese Theater.

- Bela Lugosi, famed for his portrayal of Dracula, had a photo taken with a Charlotte Clark Mickey Mouse doll on Mickey's fifth birthday in 1933 at the Hollywood Cabaret Restaurant in New York City. In 1935, he had to fill out a press biography for Cameo Pictures Corporation (where he was starring in the film *Murder by Television*) and one of the questions was his favorite film star. At first, he wrote "none" and then crossed it out and wrote "Mickey Mouse."

- In the movie *The Princess Comes Across* (1936), actress Carole Lombard played a Swedish noble woman and when reporters asked who her favorite film star was, she replied, "Meeky Mouse," always getting a huge laugh from theater audiences.

- Actress Marion Davies, the companion of newspaper magnate William Randolph Hearst, threw a Mickey Mouse party at Hearst Castle in San Simeon, California, in the 1930s where all the celebrity guests came dressed as Disney characters. Marion Davies told interviewers that she wanted to "make a motion picture with Mickey."

- Young actresses Shirley Temple and Jane Withers both had extensive collections of Mickey Mouse dolls in the mid-1930s. Shirley was an official member of the 1930s Mickey Mouse Club and proudly displayed her official certificate in a publicity photo.

- *Time* magazine for July 21, 1931, stated: "Asked, 'which is your favorite movie hero?' Miss Mary Pickford used to reply demurely: 'Mickey Mouse.'" Pickford's husband was actor Douglas Fairbanks Sr., one of the inspirations for Mickey Mouse's character.

- The *Seattle Motion Picture Record* for February 28, 1931, stated, "Word has come that Charlie Chaplin has requested that his latest production, *City Lights*, be accompanied wherever possible with a Mickey Mouse cartoon. This unusual request bears upon Chaplin's high regard for the cartoon character and surety in that his own presentation will meet with greater acclaim after an audience has been amused by Mickey's antics."

Mickey Saves Depression Businesses

For seventeen years, until he died in a plane crash in 1949, Kay Kamen handled the licensing of Disney merchandise. The May 1934 issue of *Harper's* magazine stated that Disney's "chief income from Mickey Mouse was not from films but rather from by-products."

Early in 1933, the Ingersoll-Waterbury Company of Connecticut was almost bankrupt. Kamen approved a license for them to make the first watches featuring Mickey Mouse. Kamen helped get the Mickey Mouse wristwatch featured at Macy's Department Store in New York City where 11,000 were sold in a single day when they debuted.

After only eight weeks of production, the Ingersoll-Waterbury Company had to add 2,700 employees to its existing 300 to fill the demand for the watches. By June 1935, the company reported it had sold over two-and-a-half million watches.

On May 7, 1934, the Lionel Corporation went into receivership with liquid assets of only $62,000 and liabilities of $296,000.

Kamen believed in the company and on July 19, 1934, licensed them to produce a metal wind-up handcar with Mickey and Minnie Mouse at the handles pumping up and down in a seesaw manner. It had eight sections of curved metal track to form a twenty-seven inch circle. It sold for one dollar and advertisments claimed "loaded with fun and a thousand thrills, they circle the track ten or more times at a single winding."

In four months, 253,000 sets were sold. The $296,000 owed to creditors was paid in full on December 31, 1934. On January 1, 1935, the Lionel Corporation had

$500,000 in liquid assets. It was not just the sale of the Mickey Mouse handcar but the fact that the company was associated with Mickey Mouse that made the rest of its products and the company itself popular.

In a story picked up around the world, Federal judge Guy L. Fake, who turned the financially healthy company back to its owners on January 21, 1935, gave Mickey Mouse the credit for saving it. The *New York Times* ran a headline on January 22, 1935, that stated, "Mickey Mouse Saves Jersey Toy Concern; Carries It Back to Solvency on His Railway."

A 1934 survey of seventy manufacturers of Disney character merchandise revealed that approximately ten thousand jobs had been created by the need to produce Mickey Mouse merchandise.

Mickey Comics: Uncensored Mouse

In 1989, the Mailbu Graphics group (Scott Rosenberg, Dave Olbrich, Tom Mason, Chris Ulm) was publishing the Eternity Comics line of independent black-and-white comic books that featured both original material and reprints of classic comics strips.

Comics historian Bill Blackbeard's research revealed that the copyright on some of the earliest Mickey Mouse comic strips had not been maintained. Malibu decided to reprint those strips under the title *The Uncensored Mouse*.

Each issue would have a totally black cover and nowhere on the cover or the back cover would there be a mention of Mickey Mouse. There would only be references to "a classic collection of Uncensored Floyd Gottfredson Comic Strips from the 1930s." Inside the comic book there would be the notice that "Mickey Mouse is a registered trademark of Walt Disney Productions" to demonstrate that Malibu was not trying to challenge that fact. In addition, each issue would be bagged and sealed so that a casual buyer or child couldn't flip through the comic book and mistake it for an official Disney comic book.

The Uncensored Mouse was to be published twice a month, beginning with the April 1989 issue until all the comic strips up to about the mid-1930s had been reprinted. The first issue featured the very first Mickey Mouse comic strip from January 13, 1930 (written by Walt Disney himself and drawn by Ub Iwerks), up to the March 5, 1930, strip.

The second issue reprinted the strips from March 6, 1930, to April 26, 1930. The third issue, which was prepared and ready to go to press but never printed, featured the strips from April 28, 1930, to June 18, 1930.

Originally, each of the two issues of *The Uncensored Mouse* that were published cost $2.50.

The reason the third issue never saw print was that no sooner did the first two issues appear at comic book shops than Disney filed a lawsuit claiming infringement of their character. At no time did Disney dispute that the original strips might have fallen into public domain, but they also never affirmed it.

Malibu Graphics and Disney reached an out-of-court settlement since the Disney company had enough money, enough time, and enough lawyer power to drag this suit through the courts forever. Malibu ceased publication and destroyed their remaining stock of the issues. Malibu was eventually purchased by Marvel Comics which was purchased by the Disney company. It's that circle of life thing.

Why Does Mickey's Tail Sometimes Disappear?

Officially, Mickey Mouse always has a tail, but depending upon the role he is playing or the occasion, he tucks it in to his pants.

Actually, around 1940, Mickey's tail disappeared for a period of time simply because of the labor of adding it to so many drawings when budgets were limited at the Disney studio during the war years.

Disney producer Harry Tytle said:

> Walt disliked the Mickeys drawn without tails (he called them "bob-tailed") but capitulated because he knew how much easier (and faster) this rendered the animation.

The tail is missing in cartoons like *Lend a Paw* (1941), *The Nifty Nineties* (1941), and *Mickey and the Seal* (1948), as well as the popular comic strip during this same time period.

Mickey's tail was not just a squiggly line behind him; in the early Mickey Mouse cartoons, it reacted to Mickey's moods and required a great deal of time and effort to get it right.

Author Bob Thomas recounted the story of Walt describing a fight sequence for a Mickey Mouse short, acting out all the parts for director Wilfred Jackson who did many of the early Mickey Mouse shorts. Jackson was confident that he could capture what Walt wanted.

When Walt saw the animation, he complained,

> You've got the tail all wrong. Look—Mickey's mad all over. His tail is tense, not a limp thing hanging there. What's the matter? Didn't we talk this over?

In the earliest black-and-white cartoons, Mickey often mimicked cartoon superstar Felix the Cat by using his tail to do things like grab a mallet or help reel himself up the side of a building. These type of antics disappeared in 1929 so that the tail was just an appendage, not a tool.

Mickey Mouse comic-strip artist Floyd Gottfredson recalled:

> The tail was dropped briefly during the war. It was because of the limited number of animation personnel [at the Disney studio]. They felt that it just would save some time in animation. The tail was a thing that always had to be drawn to move pretty gracefully, so it required a little attention.
>
> Then, after the war, they decided to bring it back on again and Walt asked [the comic-strip department] to reinstate the tail on Mickey, and we've had it with us ever since. I don't know whether anyone ever noticed, but as far as I know, we've never had any fan mail or comments on it.

Talking Mickey: Animators on Mickey Mouse

UB IWERKS: "Mickey was based on the character of [actor] Douglas Fairbanks Sr. He was the superhero of his day, always winning, gallant, and swashbuckling. Mickey's action was in that vein. He was always an adventurous character. I thought of him in that respect and I had him do naturally the sort of thing Doug Fairbanks would do."

DON BLUTH: "[Mickey] is an American institution, like Fred Astaire, Ginger Rogers, and Judy Garland. He's been so popular because of his personality which is similar to Charlie Chaplin's Little Tramp—the innocent little fool the world crushes. People like him because he believes that things will work out."

RALPH BAKSHI: "Mickey Mouse's popularity is due to the integrity of how he was animated. He is a very beautifully designed character. That's what keeps him alive. Walt loved him and that shows."

GLEN KEANE: "Mickey takes a leap forward whenever an animator makes him his own and isn't afraid of flexing the design a little to personalize him. The worst thing for animators is to be afraid of Mickey so they don't put something of themselves into him. If you approach him too reverently, you end up with a lifeless, stiff icon, instead of a real flesh-and-blood character."

MARK HENN: "There are definitely limits to the character. He's a hero. He represents all the good things in people. Just to say he's a good guy who would never hurt a fly is too extreme. Mickey is a character with difficult proportions to render. And if you don't do it really well, if his nose is too big, or his ears are off, it jumps out at you. Mickey is very easy to draw...badly."

ANDREAS DEJA: "The hardest thing about animating Mickey...is that the whole world knows him and how he behaves. You really have to go back and study the old shorts to find out what these characters are all about. It's not just how he looks or moves, but what is in his soul that makes him so incredibly appealing. Mickey Mouse represents the world of animation...and I think every animator at one time or another would love to draw him."

MARC DAVIS: "Mickey became the straight man, the average guy, and the average guy is never as interesting as the flamboyant character (like Donald Duck). Yet, he has lived all this time, and is perhaps one of the greatest folk characters of all time."

WILLIE ITO: "We've grown up with Mickey and his particular personality. In his black and white days, he was a mischievous little boy. Then he grew up to be the guy next door—adventurous and slightly mischievous, but a right fellow, never out to hurt anyone and never cruel. He's a wholesome character."

OLLIE JOHNSTON: "I liked doing Mickey because he was more like Walt. He'd win his battle using his head and his wits, while the duck would just get mad and throw things. I didn't like working on Donald. Mickey had more depth to his personality. Mickey was more intelligent. We always thought Mickey was Walt's alter ego. I loved Fred Moore's drawings of Mickey. He was the greatest Mickey man."

FLOYD NORMAN: "In a very real way, Mickey Mouse is Walt Disney, the scrappy little guy who maintains a positive attitude no matter how bad things get. Mickey Mouse is intrepid, resourceful and optimistic to a fault. The famous mouse continues to reflect the core values of Walt's mission even though today's successful corporation often disappoints. Mickey Mouse is a continual reminder we can all be better than we are."

Mickey Comics: Mickey Attempts Suicide

In 1920, Walt Disney saw a Harold Lloyd silent theatrical comedy entitled *Haunted Spooks* where Lloyd's character tries to kill himself. Being a comedy, Lloyd picks up a gun to shoot himself and it turns out to be a water pistol. He stands in front of a trolley to be run over and it veers away on another track a mere three feet in front of him.

In the Mickey Mouse comic-strip story *Mr. Slicker and the Egg Robbers* (September 22, 1930, through December 29, 1930), written by Floyd Gottfredson, who was also drawing the strip, Gottfredson got a suggestion from Walt that he discussed in a November 1975 interview:

> [Walt] would make suggestions every once in a while, for some short continuities and so on, and I would do them. One that I'll never forget, and which I still don't understand, was when he said, "Why don't you do a continuity of Mickey trying to commit suicide?"
> So I said, "Walt! You're kidding!" He replied, "No, I'm not kidding. I think you could get a lot of funny stuff out of that." I said, "Gee whiz, Walt. I don't know. What do you think the [King Features] Syndicate will think of it? What do you think the editors will think? And the readers?"
> He said, "I think it will be funny. Go ahead and do it." So I did, oh, maybe ten days of Mickey trying to commit suicide (roughly from October 8 through October 24, 1930)—jumping off bridges, trying to hang himself. ... I don't remember all the details. But strangely enough, the syndicate didn't object. We didn't hear anything from the editors, and Walt said, "See? It was funny. I told you it would be."

Thinking Minnie is in love with someone else Mickey tries jumping off a high bridge but lands instead on the deck of a small boat that had been tugging underneath.

Mickey turns on the gas in his house but a squirrel scampers in to use the escaping gas to over-inflate his balloon that explodes and scares Mickey. Mickey puts a huge anvil around his neck and goes to the river bank where the fish tell him the water is freezing, so Mickey decides against it.

Mickey soon discovers that his fears were unfounded. Minnie loves only him and he was mistaken. Mickey never again contemplated suicide as a solution.

However, this is not the end of the story. The first-ever Disney book published for retail purposes in the United Kingdom was the *Mickey Mouse Annual* from London's Dean and Sons Limited around Christmas of 1930. In the third volume in 1932, cartoonist Wilfred Haughton did an original one-page strip with Mickey entitled "A Close Shave."

Mickey is shocked to see in the distance, at a park, Minnie sitting on a bench next to a top-hat wearing male mouse. Mickey immediately assumes that Minnie has found a new boyfriend. In a nearby shop he buys a revolver and a lengthy coil of rope to end it all.

After rowing into a lake, he ties a noose around his neck and ties the other end to a low, overhanging branch of a tree. When he fires the gun, he pushes the rowboat away so he will also hang, but because of the action, the shot misses his head and severs the rope hanging from the tree.

Mickey falls into the shallow lake. "It is a jolly good job I can swim, or I should have drowned!"

Mickey Imposter: Mickey in Vietnam

Mickey Mouse in Vietnam was the work of Lee Savage (father of *Mythbusters* Adam Savage) and Milton Glaser (who designed the I ♥ New York logo) for the Angry Arts Festival in 1968. The festival was designed to give creative artists a forum for protesting the Vietnam War.

The silent, 16mm black-and-white cartoon that lasts a little over a minute was officially titled *Short Subject*. It finds the early 1929 version of Mickey Mouse happily walking along. He passes a billboard that reads, "Join the Army and See the World." Mickey studies the billboard, walks off-screen, and then returns wearing a helmet and carrying a military rifle with a bayonet.

Mickey sails off on a tugboat (so small that he is the only passenger) with the words "To Vietnam" printed along the bow. The voyage is unusually quick, with Mickey sailing across a calm Pacific Ocean from the USA (which is helpfully identified by a large sign posted on its shoreline) to Vietnam (which has its own large sign on its shore, along with huge explosions popping all over its land mass). Mickey arrives and marches into Vietnam, following an arrow-shaped sign that reads, "War Zone."

Mickey is barely a few seconds into an overgrown jungle when he suddenly drops his rifle, goes stiff, and falls over backwards. The camera finds him flat on the ground, with a bullet hole in his skull. Mickey's smiling face turns glum as blood trickles out of the bullet hole. That's the entire film.

Savage, who is credited as director and animator of the short, and Glaser offered private screenings during the early 1970s. The film occasionally popped up in film festivals but was not widely known among Disney fans and was never released theatrically.

Glaser said:

> Mickey Mouse is a symbol of innocence, and of America, and of success, and of idealism. And to have him killed, as a solider, is such a contradiction of your expectations. And when you're dealing with communication, when you contradict expectations, you get a result.

The Disney company made no attempt to destroy copies of the film, but neither did it give the film any public recognition. Glaser remembers there was some talk about Disney suing them, but he was told it didn't happen because Disney didn't want to attract any attention to the film and felt it wouldn't be able to recover sufficient financial penalties to justify the time and expense.

Voting for Mickey Mouse

Voters will protest the candidates (especially in presidential elections) given to them on a ballot by writing in the name of a celebrity or fictitious character instead. However, most states can not officially count votes for uncertified candidates since they require potential write-in candidates to register.

Mickey Mouse is perhaps the best-known and most frequently used as a write-in candidate. The earliest known documentation of Mickey Mouse as a write-in candidate was in the 1932 New York mayoral elections.

It has been estimated that Mickey Mouse can get up to as many as 20,000 votes in an election year as a write-in candidate for some office. In the November 2014 election in Orange County in Florida, Mickey Mouse pulled in 273 votes for positions ranging from governor to commissioner of agriculture.

In the 2008 county elections in Sheboygan, Wisconsin, Mickey received four votes for coroner, two for state representative, and one each for governor, clerk of court, and county clerk. In the 2008 presidential election, Mickey received eleven votes nationally, beating out write-ins for Joe the Plumber, Jesus Christ, and Santa Claus.

Elections Supervisor Gail Whitehead of Savannah, Georgia, said in 2012:

> Mickey always gets votes. If he doesn't get votes in our election, it's a bad election.

Where Do The Stories Come From? 'Traffic Troubles' (1931)

Traffic Troubles features Mickey as a reckless taxi driver with an anthropomorphic cab. His first passenger is a large pig who he loses on a road full of potholes when he bounces out of the cab. His second fare is Minnie on her way to a music lesson. Problems arise when Pete's elixir is poured into the gas tank and the car goes out of control. Mickey is also confronted by a police officer who asks many questions but silences him at the same time when he tries to answer.

Ben Sharpsteen, who directed many of the earliest Disney cartoons including this one, recalled,

> In the early days, when we were making animated shorts, Walt was driving through town and was stopped by a cop, who gave him a ticket. He returned to the studio and told us about it. He re-enacted his conversation with the cop in a way that revealed he did not think it was very funny.
>
> Each time he told the story, however, it became funnier, and his attitude changed. Parts of the story were added and others eliminated. One of Walt's strengths was not just creating a story but editing it, refining it. And before we knew it, we were starting a Mickey Mouse picture called *Traffic Troubles* that turned out pretty good.

Are Mickey and Minnie Married?

Officially, the Disney company states that Mickey and Minnie are not married. Being married is an adult thing to do and Mickey and Minnie are not adults despite driving cars, owning homes, having adult jobs, and other activities.

Walt Disney said in 1933:

> What it amounts to is that Minnie is, for screen purposes, his leading lady. If the story calls for a romantic courtship, then Minnie is the girl; but when the story requires a married couple, then they appear as man and wife. In the studio, we have decided that they are married really.

A conservative, moral man, it is doubtful that Walt would tolerate his alter-ego dating his girlfriend for decades with no marriage plans. It is more likely that Walt considered Mickey and Minnie to be just like other popular performing couples in the 1930s, such as George Burns and Gracie Allen or Jack Benny and Mary Livingstone, who were married in real life but on the radio and in the movies often appeared as being single.

The general public considered Mickey and Minnie already married, with songs like *The Wedding Party of Mickey Mouse* (1931) and *The Wedding of Mister Mickey Mouse* (1933) both approved by the Disney studio and featuring Disney-created artwork reinforcing the matrimony.

Of course, in the cartoon *Mickey's Nightmare* (1932), Mickey dreams of getting married to Minnie and the bliss it will bring. However, Mickey is so inundated with a never-ending stream of baby mice and their many demands that the dream becomes a nightmare.

An abandoned Mickey Mouse short in 1941 was entitled *Mickey's Elopement* where Mickey is trying to get Minnie to an all-night wedding chapel.

Actress Russi Taylor, who provided the voice of Minnie Mouse starting in 1986, was married to the late voice actor Wayne Allwine who performed the voice of Mickey Mouse. So, for a while, it was true that Mickey and Minnie were happily married in real life.

Taylor said in 1997:

> The characters aren't going to get married, because children relate to Mickey and Minnie at their own levels. They don't know how old Mickey and Minnie are, but if they were to get married, they would become adults and spoil the illusion.

Walt realized that as well and told the *News Chronicle* in June 1935 that "there's no marriage in the land of make-believe. Mickey and Minnie must live happily ever after."

The Mickey Mouse Club Creed

It was common for kids to join fan clubs for their favorite cowboy western stars and the serial heroes they heard weekly on radio, so it was no surprise that Mickey Mouse had his own similar fan club.

In September 1929, Harry W. Woodin approached Walt Disney with the idea of a movie theater-sponsored club for boys and girls that would be centered on a Mickey Mouse meeting every Saturday morning. It became so popular that it expanded into theaters across the country and lasted until around 1935.

On the back of each membership card, just like other fan club cards, was a set of high standards expected of every member:

> I will be a square shooter in my home, in school, on the playgrounds, wherever I may be.
> I will be truthful and honorable and strive always to make myself a better and more useful little citizen.
> I will respect my elders and help the aged, the helpless and children smaller than myself.
> In short, I will be a good American!

At meetings, club members would recite the MMC creed as part of the meeting and then repeat the Mickey Mouse Club Pledge: "Mickey Mice do not swear, smoke, cheat, or lie."

The Mouse That Ate Public Domain

In 2003, the cartoon *Steamboat Willie* was finally about to enter public domain. The copyright had been repeatedly extended by acts of Congress several times, oddly at roughly the same moment the film was to enter the public domain.

In 2003, due to aggressive lobbying and donations by the Disney company, the Copyright Term Extension Act was passed extending the copyright of *Steamboat Willie* once again, this time to the year 2024. It is often referred to in a derogatory manner as the "Mickey Mouse Protection Act."

Of course, Mickey Mouse is also a trademarked character and trademarks can be kept alive indefinitely as long as they are in use commercially and aggressively defended. So, while a particular early cartoon like *Steamboat Willie* may eventually fall into public domain, the Disney company can legitimately argue that Mickey Mouse as a character cannot be used by others as long as the trademark is in force and by doing so may cause "confusion in the marketplace."

Walt filed his application to trademark Mickey Mouse with the U.S. Patent Office on May 21, 1928, and the trademark was granted the following September 18, 1928, which may also explain why that month was sometimes used as Mickey's birthday month.

Mickey Cartoons: Ten Mickey Cartoons Never Made

Animator and director Jack Hannah said:

> Mickey was a little more the hero type so it was a little bit harder to find material for him. Walt had a special love for Mickey and I don't think he wanted to see Mickey roughed up so we struggled to come up with story ideas.

Here are some never developed proposals from the 1930s at the height of Mickey's popularity:

- "Navy Mickey": Mickey joins the navy (just like Roy O. Disney did during World War I) and has run-ins with an admiral who is a bulldog.
- "Hillbilly Mickey": In the mountains, moonshiner Pete mistakes newcomer Mickey as a "revenuer" sent to close down his still.
- "Jungle Mickey": Mickey as a newsreel photographer in darkest Africa.
- "Pilgrim Mickey": This would have been the only Thanksgiving short ever made by the Disney studio. There were several variations on the story, including Mickey recounting a tall tale to his nephews of how he went hunting for a turkey and ran into Indian trouble.
- "Tanglefoot": Taking place at a racetrack, Mickey is the owner of a horse with hay fever named Tanglefoot. At the time, Walt owned polo ponies and wanted to develop the personality of the horse as a supporting character since Horace Horsecollar was now a pseudo-human like Goofy.

- "Pluto's Robot Twin": Mickey builds a robot dog to show Pluto how a good dog should behave. Unfortunately, the robot goes out of control and Pluto must rescue Mickey from the berserk automaton.
- "Mickey's Toothache": Because of an aching tooth, Mickey takes ether at the dentist and falls asleep. He dreams that Dentist Pete takes him to court (where a gigantic wisdom tooth is the judge) and charges Mickey with dental neglect. Mickey confronts creatures that are half animal and half dental instruments in a nightmarish world. Disney artists spent six months coming up with elaborate pencil drawings.
- "Prehistoric Mickey": The story of caveman Mickey Mouse and dinosaurs.
- "Mickey's Follies": Mickey is the host for an elaborate musical revue like the famous Ziegfeld Follies featuring all the standard Disney characters as well as some of the popular ones from the Silly Symphonies.
- "Mickey's Hotel": There were at least two versions of this story. One had Goofy and Donald as bumbling bellboys. Another had Mickey running his hotel with robots which, like all robots in animated cartoons, go out of control.

Talking Mickey: Walt on Mickey's Personality

"Sometimes I've tried to figure out why Mickey appealed to the whole world. Everybody's tried to figure it out. So far as I know, nobody has. He's a pretty nice fellow who never does anybody any harm, who gets into scrapes through no fault of his own, but always manages to come up grinning. Why, Mickey's even been faithful to one girl, Minnie, all his life. Mickey is so simple and uncomplicated, so easy to understand that you can't help liking him.

"We learned after hard lessons, too, that the public wants its heroes. In some of the pictures we tried to let other animals steal the honors from Mickey. There was an immediate reaction against this. He had become a hero in the eyes of his audiences, especially the youngsters. Mickey could do no wrong. I could never attribute any meanness or callow traits to him.

"Back in those days, when I was making nothing but the Mickey [cartoons], I always thought of him as a personality. There were things that he would do and there were things that he just couldn't do. I would think of it this way, 'Now this is something that Mickey could do.' I never thought of him as a mouse. We thought of him more as a little boy.

"I compared him to [comedian] Harold Lloyd. Mickey in himself wasn't funny. He was cute. So the situation had to make Mickey funny.

"He is never mean or ugly. He never lies nor cheats nor steals. He is a clean, happy, little fellow who loves life and folks. He never takes advantage of the weak.

"We kept him loveable although ludicrous in his blundering heroics. And that's the way he's remained despite any outside influences. He's grown into a consistent, predictable character to whom we could assign only the kind of role and antics which were correct for his reputation.

"Instead of speeding up the cartoons, as was then the fashion, we were not afraid to slow down the tempo and let Mickey emote. We allowed audiences to get acquainted with him. To recognize him as a personality.

"The Mouse's private life isn't especially colorful. He's never been the type that would go in for swimming pools and night clubs, more the simple country boy at heart. Lives on a quiet residential street, has occasional dates with his girl friend, Minnie, doesn't drink or smoke, likes the movies and band concerts, things like that."

Men Behind the Mouse: Ub Iwerks

Ubbe Eert Iwwerks (who legally shortened his Dutch name to Ub Iwerks in 1926) was an animator and inventor who worked with Walt Disney for much of his life. He was a shy, sometimes inarticulate, serious fellow whose talent amazed everyone.

He was born March 14, 1901, and died July 7, 1971.

Iwerks was the second father to Mickey Mouse and has been referred to as "the hand behind the mouse." He was the best draftsman at the Disney studio and one who could turn out the most footage. He could do 600–700 usable drawings a day which translated into roughly one drawing a minute during a ten-hour day.

Walt and Iwerks became friends as teenagers. It was Iwerks who came up with the actual final design of Mickey Mouse based on Walt's ideas and was the person who virtually animated all of the first three Mickey Mouse films by himself.

Dave Iwerks, Ub's son, shared in a 1978 interview:

> Mickey was not born on that [train] ride, as per legend. He was created at a drawing board in Los Angeles. Father drew many characters, one of which was a mouse. He wasn't one to boast "Look what I did!" It was all in his day's work. He said it didn't matter who first drew Mickey but what Walt did with the character that was really important.
>
> Dad did everything on the first three Mickey cartoons, from the first stroke on the drawing board to the finished cartoon. Proof of Dad's importance to Walt lies in the fact that in 1930, Dad earned $150 a week while Walt collected $75. Reason Dad got twice as much as Walt was because Walt wanted to keep Dad there at all costs. He understood his value.

Iwerks illustrated the first three weeks of the Mickey Mouse comic strip as well as many promotional items featuring Mickey Mouse including a giveaway phenakistoscope of Mickey walking forward.

He left the Disney studio in January 1930 to start his own animation studio, for a variety of reasons, including some personal disagreements with Walt.

Iwerks returned to the Disney studio in 1940 but not to animation. He developed the Special Process Laboratory that handled primarily photographic processes, such as special effects for both animation and live action, winning him two special Oscars for these achievements.

The First Mickey Mouse Ride

Disney merchandise executive Kay Kamen worked with the largest store retailers around the United States at Christmas time to guarantee that they featured a Disney theme for their Toyland areas during the holiday season.

In 1935, he arranged for the publication of a softcover Big Little Book that was 148 pages in length with black-and-white illustrations entitled *Mickey Mouse and the Magic Carpet*. It told the adventures of Mickey and his friends as they climbed aboard "an ancient carpet from out of the east, from the land of the Arabian nights" that took Mickey and his friends across North America to destinations like the Grand Canyon and Niagara Falls.

As Disney historian David Lesjak discovered, the book was connected with an interactive ride that retailers could purchase directly from Kamen.

The 1935 merchandising manual indicated:

> In groups as large as fifty, [children] are seated on a carpet 30 feet long by 6 feet wide...on goes a cloud machine...a wind machine...and a whirring motor sound to simulate an airplane. On a translucent screen is flashed...motion pictures depicting a trip over mountains, snow, etc. The carpet...starts an undulating motion...pronounced enough to give the effect of a ride through the air.

At the conclusion of the ride, children visited Santa and received a copy of the book only available at that store.

Keeps On Ticking

- The very first Mickey Mouse Ingersoll wristwatch was featured at the Century of Progress Exposition in Chicago in 1933 where it outsold the World's Fair commemorative watch by a three-to-one margin, often selling five thousand watches a day, usually to adults who stood in long lines to purchase one.

- At the 1939 New York World's Fair, A.W. Robertson, chairman of the board of Westinghouse, and Grover Whalen, president of the 1939 New York World's Fair, placed a Mickey Mouse wristwatch into a sealed time capsule not to be opened for five thousand years (the year 6939).

- In 1968, comedian Bill ("Jose Jimenez") Dana gave his new Mickey Mouse wristwatch to astronaut Walter Schirra, who carried it with him on the Apollo 7 spacecraft that orbited the Earth. Astronaut Eugene Cernan wore his Mickey Mouse watch given to him by the commander of the Blue Angels during the 1969 Apollo 10 mission that went to the moon.

- On Wednesday, March 27, 1957, at Disneyland, California, U.S. Time (Timex Corporation) officials presented Walt Disney with the 25-millionth Mickey Mouse watch. By 1946 U.S. Time had absorbed the Ingersoll-Waterbury Clock Company but continued to display the Ingersoll brand on Mickey Mouse watches until 1948.

Mickey Military Insignia

During World War II, the Disney studio provided hundreds of insignia designs for various branches of the U.S. armed services.

While no official numbers were kept, Mickey Mouse appeared on less than three dozen and generally for units like the signal corps, home-front activities, or a chaplain's unit. He was considered too nice a guy to appear aggressive. Donald Duck, because of his more feisty personality, appeared on almost two hundred insignias.

Unapproved Mickey Mouse insignias were even displayed on Nazi warcraft.

A prominent and feared Mickey Mouse insignia first appeared around 1937 when German flying ace Adolf Galland of the Luftwaffe painted a homemade version of Mickey on all the fighters he flew. A demonic-looking Mickey had a cigar in his mouth and held a pistol in one hand and an axe in the other. When asked why he chose Mickey Mouse, Galland replied, "I like Mickey Mouse. I always have. And I like cigars, but I had to give them up after the war."

Hundreds of German U-boat submarines displayed emblems on their bows during the war. They varied from typical war emblems of swords, axes, and torpedoes to Mickey Mouse with an umbrella on U-26 that served from 1936 to July 1940 and sank eleven ships.

Mickey Comics: DeMolay Mickey

Walt Disney joined the DeMolay Kansas City Chapter run by Frank S. "Dad" Land in 1920. The Masonic youth group allowed boys aged twelve to twenty-one to share common interests and learn responsibility and other skills, while being mentored by business professionals.

Walt received the DeMolay Legion of Honor in October 1931 for outstanding leadership. He had studio artist Les Clark draw a special full-color picture of Mickey proudly wearing a DeMolay medal for Land.

Walt also arranged for Disney animator Fred Spencer, another alummus of DeMolay, to produce a monthly Mickey Mouse two-tier black-and-white comic strip for the *International DeMolay Cordon* newsletter. Spencer, who prominently signed the artwork, had worked on the early Mickey Mouse cartoons.

The Mickey Mouse Chapter strip appeared December 1932 through May 1933 (except March 1933) for a total of five installments before it stopped without explanation. The strip depicted the happenings in the DeMolay Chapter formed by Mickey and his barnyard friends including Horace Horsecollar. Since DeMolay was just for boys, there were no female characters. One episode had Pluto chasing a cat and disrupting a DeMolay meeting chaired by Mickey.

Walt Disney was never a Mason, though some authors have misinterpreted his involvement with DeMolay and his wearing a DeMolay ring for years as proof that he was.

Mickey Cartoons: 'The Plight of the Bumblebee'

It was not unusual for an animated short to be started but then abandoned because of crowd scenes too expensive to animate or necessary special effects.

In 1951, one Mickey Mouse cartoon was over ninety percent animated before it was stopped. Entitled *The Plight of the Bumblebee* as a take-off on the name of the famous musical piece "Flight of the Bumblebee," the primary Mickey Mouse animation was done by Fred Moore, with other scenes animated by Cliff Nordberg and Hal King. John Sibley was involved as well.

The short was directed by Jack Kinney, who stated:

> The best Mickey ever was never finished. It was called *The Plight of the Bumblebee*, and it was all finished in animation. It had an awkward length, but Fred and Sib agreed that it could not be cut, so it was shelved.

The cartoon was done with a straight announcer voice-over narration probably by Wendell Niles, Ken Niles' brother, since Mickey's voice, because of its limited range, could not sustain long stretches of dialog. The singer sounds a bit like Bill Roberts in places, and the female character sounds like Aileen Carlisle.

The storyline is that a disheveled Mickey dressed in a suburban suit like Don Draper stumbles into a local bar, where he finds a bee named Hector singing "bebop" (a bee who is jazz bopping), but notices that the bee occasionally hits a beautiful operatic note. Mickey decides the bee is destined for bigger things, and becomes his manager by signing Hector to a contract. However, Mickey soon discovers that the reason Hector is singing in a bar is that he has a weakness for the nectar of flowers.

In fact, whenever he has a drink of nectar, he becomes a sloppy drunk. So, Mickey tries to keep Hector away from all temptation. Unfortunately, for Hector's operatic debut, the stage set is decorated with flowers and Hector overindulges, causing the female opera diva on stage to go into a fit and faint at his behavior. Chaos ensues. After the performance, a defeated Mickey runs across a musical grasshopper outside and decides to try again.

The premise is very similar to other animated cartoons, like *Dixieland Droopy* (MGM 1954), *One Froggy Evening* (Warners 1955), and *Finnegan's Flea* (Paramount 1958).

In 1981, artist Daan Jippes, who was working at the Disney studio in Burbank in Consumer Products, found some information about Production 2428 (*The Plight of the Bumblebee),* including the location of three dusty boxes filled with stacks of animation, layouts, photographed storyboards, and x-sheets (exposure sheets). He also found the recorded soundtrack (with the final voices) on a transcription disc.

Disney artist Floyd Gottfredson, who did the Mickey Mouse comic strip, stated:

> This big model sheet up here that I use as reference was all made from drawings that [Fred Moore] made for *The Plight of the Bumblebee*. Mickey had a bee that could buzz operatic numbers; he was a great virtuoso that way.
>
> But the bee had a weakness; he was a nectarholic: he'd get drunk on nectar, so Mickey had trouble controlling him this way. Fred got that picture about 90% animated, I understand, and Walt dumped it because he got scared of the alcoholic connotations.

The alcoholic connotation was probably not the reason, because during this time period, drunkenness was not considered a disease but a weakness and often a springboard for comedic moments in films.

Under the supervision of animator and director Burny Mattinson and using all the elements that had been found, a picture reel was filmed and shown to Disney executives but Jeffrey Katzenberg passed on completing it.

Mickey's Nephews: Morty and Ferdie

Morty and Ferdie (sometimes spelled "Ferdy"), Mickey's twin mischievous nephews, first appeared in September 18, 1932, in the Mickey Mouse Sunday newspaper comic strip. Morty is short for "Mortimer" and Ferdie is short for "Ferdinand."

Their mother, Mrs. Fieldmouse, asks Mickey to baby sit them while she runs an errand and never returns, just like Donald's sister who disappeared after leaving her three young sons with Donald Duck. The reason for introducing nephews was to give writers more possible springboards for stories. Instead of being a stern parent, both Mickey and Donald could be more forgiving and fun as uncles.

Officially, Mickey's nephews appear together (with Shirley Reed supplying their voices) in only one theatrical animated short, *Mickey's Steam-Roller* (1934), although they were frequently featured in comic books and storybooks. They did have a very brief cameo in a crowd scene in *Boat Builders* (1938).

As Mickey Mouse authority David Gerstein has pointed out, as early as *Giantland* (1933) the horde of orphan mice in the Mickey Mouse cartoons were referred to as "nephews" in story conferences, though never identified as such in the actual films or storybooks. Mickey's nephews never achieved the popularity or appealing personality of Donald Duck's nephews Huey, Dewey, and Louie.

The Disney Channel's New Mickey Mouse Cartoons

A new series of Mickey Mouse cartoons premiered on the Disney Channel on June 28, 2013. Chris Diamantopoulos provides the voice of Mickey Mouse rather than the official voice, Bret Iwan, because the producer wanted a voice with more "edge."

Executive producer and director Paul Rudish said:

> The immediate inspiration for the new Mickey Mouse shorts is—the old Mickey Mouse shorts! The originals were kind of our launching point, to go back to that flavor of Mickey. As long as his personality is intact, Mickey can live and do anything all over the world.
>
> Drawing a historic character like Mickey has been an honor, a little bit intimidating, but ultimately fun! I was raised on Disney cartoons, as most kids are even today, I think. Mickey was an inspiration to me early on, so to be able to follow in the footsteps of artists who have been so inspirational to me, to follow the trail that Walt and Ub Iwerks blazed, has been a remarkable opportunity.

The cartoons are done using a Flash animation program called Harmony with backgrounds done in Photoshop. There was a thirty-person team in Burbank and an animation team in Canada.

The cartoons run three-and-a-half minutes each. Each one finds Mickey in a different modern setting, such as Santa Monica, New York, Paris, Beijing, Tokyo, Venice, and the Alps, facing a silly situation, a quick complication, and an escalation of physical visual gags before the conclusion.

Senior Vice President Eric Coleman at Disney Television Animation said:

> The goal is to introduce Mickey to a new generation of kids and at the same time entertain their parents who have their memories of Mickey Mouse. Our intention is

to highlight his personality and show him as the star he has always been.

Making them feel contemporary doesn't mean give them an iPhone and headphones; it's the execution, the sensibility, the tone, the way they are animated, the music, the movement, the timing, the editing. We wanted to make shorts that would play well globally. We have Disney Channels around the world.

Season five (in 2018) takes the series total to more than 90 shorts, including a special seven-minute extended-length birthday episode airing in late 2018. The twenty-one minute long *Duck the Halls: A Mickey Mouse Christmas Special* was released in 2016.

The series also inspired Mickey and Minnie's Runaway Railway, an attraction coming to Disney's Hollywood Studios in 2019.

Guests will enter the Chinese Theater for a premiere of a new Mickey Mouse cartoon short featuring a new song. In the pre-show, guests see Mickey and Minnie getting ready for a picnic and as they drive there, they pass alongside of a train with Goofy as the engineer.

The attraction puts the guests on Goofy's train using trackless technology as they enter the cartoon itself. Suddenly guests find themselves in the middle of a stampede followed by a trip to a carnival that ends in being caught up in a twister.

The whirling wind drops everyone into a tropical locale with a large screen and water effects (since the train cars are teetering near the edge of a waterfall). Those cars flush through a drainage pipe into a big city where there is a dance studio run by an audio-animatronic Daisy Duck who even gets the cars to dance.

Somehow all of this leads to an alleyway with a large factory where Mickey and Minnie must save the guests from a giant furnace before arriving in the park for the picnic. The guests go out through a movie screen to get to the final exit.

Why Does Mickey Wear White Gloves and Big Shoes?

Walt told author Bob Thomas:
> [Mickey's] legs were pipe stems, and we stuck them in big shoes to give him the look of a kid wearing his father's shoes.

Mickey first wore shoes in *Gallopin' Gaucho* (1928). The shoes also hid Mickey's real feet so he appeared more human and less like an animal.

Walt continued:
> We didn't want him to have mouse hands, because he was supposed to be more human. So we gave him gloves. Artistically five digits are too many for a mouse. His hand would look like a bunch of bananas. Financially, not having an extra finger in each of the 45,000 drawings to animate for a short has saved the studio millions.

Every time Mickey's gloveless, black-colored hand moved across his solid black torso, his hand just disappeared, so white gloves made it easier for audiences to see and to allow Mickey more expression with his hands.

The three black lines that sometime appear on the backs of the gloves represent darts in the gloves' fabric extending from between the digits of the hand, typical of the design style of a child's glove from the 1930s. Mickey first wore his white gloves on screen in the short *The Opry House* (1929).

Where Do the Stories Come From? 'Mickey's Kangaroo' (1935)

In *Mickey's Kangaroo*, Mickey receives a crate from Australia sent by a "Leo Buring" that contains a boxing kangaroo and its baby. These new arrivals make Pluto angry when they destroy his new doghouse and jealous when Mickey pays so much attention to them.

Mickey gets his boxing gloves and cheerfully battles the adult in his improvised boxing ring. This was the last black-and-white Mickey Mouse cartoon made during Walt's lifetime and one of the longest at nine minutes. This short inspired a similar storyline in the Mickey Mouse comic strip a few months later.

In 1934, an Australian admirer of Walt Disney, wine-maker Leo Buring, shipped Walt a crate with the gift of two wallabies, a male and a female. By the time they arrived in California, they had given birth to a child. The Disney staff, inspired by the names of the Marx Brothers, named them Leapo (the male), Hoppo (the female), and Poucho (the baby).

The wallabies were kept in a pen outside the story department to be used for live-action reference sketching by the animators. They were later donated to a zoo.

Who Does Mickey Mouse's Voice?

Officially, there have only been five people who provided the voice for Mickey Mouse. Walt Disney himself and later sound effects man Jimmy MacDonald and his apprentice Wayne Allwine were the first three.

Beginning in 2009, Bret Iwan is the official voice of Mickey Mouse, though Chris Diamantopoulos does the voice in the series of new Disney Channel shorts because the producer wanted an "edgier" sounding Mickey.

Mickey's creator Walt Disney spoke for the little fellow from 1928 to 1947, as well as supplying Mickey's voice for animated portions of the original *Mickey Mouse Club* television show in the mid-1950s.

Disney sound effects man Jimmy MacDonald took over from 1947 (beginning with *Mickey and the Beanstalk*) to 1976. Wayne Allwine, who had been assisting MacDonald with sound effects, performed the vocalizations from 1977 to 2009.

There is so much need for the famous falsetto that several uncredited performers have also done Mickey's voice. Joe Twerp supplied the voice for seventeen episodes of the *Mickey Mouse Theater of the Air* in the 1930s.

Comedian and writer Stan Freberg supplied the voice on a 1955 children's record, *Mickey Mouse's Birthday Party*. Jack Wagner, the voice of Disneyland, often did Mickey's voice for various theme park-related events like parades and announcements. Pete Renaday filled in after Wagner died.

Carl Stalling and Clarence "Ducky" Nash stepped in during the early cartoons to cover a line or two when Walt wasn't available.

Les Perkins did the voice of Mickey in the 1987 television special *Down and Out with Donald Duck* as well as the

DTV Valentine in 1986. Quinton Flynn did Mickey's voice in some episodes of the 1999 television series *Mickey Mouse Works*.

That incomplete list doesn't even include all the different foreign voice artists who supplied Mickey's voice in different languages for overseas releases over the decades.

MacDonald recalled:

> Giving an hour or two every now and then to record [Mickey's] lines. That's all. It's not a full-time job. He never had much dialog. If you can get your voice into a falsetto you can pretty much do it. Problem is, if you do it too long, you go hoarse.

Allwine stated:

> I've been privileged to voice Mickey for nearly 30 years, but he's not just a voice to me. You can't work with Mickey without it changing you. I'm a better person for having done his voice.

Mickey's Voice: Walt Disney

A talented and humorous natural performer, Walt Disney was the first person to supply voices for Disney animated cartoons, including using his theatrical skills to bring an extra dimension to Mickey's personality.

He told interviewer Tony Thomas in 1959:

> We were foolin' around and tryin' to get a voice for a mouse. And we didn't know what a mouse would sound like, so I said, "It's kind of like this." And the guys said "Well, why don't you do it?" And I knew I'd always be on the payroll, so I did it.

Walt would often ad-lib dialog for Mickey in that well-known voice resulting in appreciative laughter from his listeners.

In the earliest cartoons, Mickey squeaked and squawked. His first words were not uttered until *The Karnival Kid* (1929) where as a carnival hot dog vendor he gleefully shouts, "Hot dog! Hot dog!" (Not "hot dogs!" plural.)

At one point, Walt felt his Midwestern twang and lack of professional acting experience might hamper Mickey Mouse's success, so he spent a week auditioning professional actors to take over the part. Despite Walt's impassioned coaching and the best efforts of these performers, no one was able to capture Mickey's intrepid optimism and pluck as deftly as Walt himself.

Walt often told others that he preferred his unique vocal interpretation because "there is more pathos in it."

Author Bob Thomas said:

> It was no easy matter to get color into such an unnatural, limited voice, but Walt managed. No one else could capture the gulping, ingenuous, half-brave quality like he did so well.

Disney producer Harry Tytle recalled:

> Part of Walt's preference for the sparing use of dialog [with Mickey Mouse] could have been that it was less time-consuming for him. In later years, others did the voice, but we also had a film library of Walt's Mickey Mouse lines to fall back on. Walt was generally so involved in other work that he was not available on short notice. Then, too, the falsetto voice was not an easy thing for him to do in later years.

Wayne Allwine, one of the official voices for Mickey Mouse, said:

> Walt was a high baritone. His constant smoking dried out his vocal chords over time so it brought down the pitch and you could hear the difference.

Mickey's Voice: Jimmy MacDonald

Jimmy MacDonald invented many of the Disney sound effects, building over five hundred contraptions in his home workshop. Walt originally recorded Mickey's dialog for *Mickey and the Beanstalk* (1947) in May 1940, but production on the film was continually delayed and the story frequently rewritten, requiring Walt to return over the years to the sound stage to record the new lines.

MacDonald remembered:

> I started doing Mickey's voice when we were doing *Mickey and the Beanstalk*. The director kept needing Walt to do Mickey. He said, "I'm too busy, I just can't do it. Call Jim up here."
>
> They said, "Walt wants to see you," and I thought, 'What have I done now?' He said, "Have you ever tried to do Mickey?" I said, "No, Walt." You wouldn't try to do that, because it was always Walt's voice; there was no reason ever to try it. So he said, "Do it. Just say something." So I said [in Mickey's voice], "Hi, Walt, how are you?" You know, Mickey always had that little identifiable giggle.

A test recording was done of MacDonald trying to match the vocal track Walt had done five years earlier. They were compared and Walt was pleased that MacDonald had captured Mickey's spirit and limited vocal range.

MacDonald recalled:

> Walt said, "That's fine." He told the directors, "Have Jim do it in the future. He can do it fine." But he told me, "Don't let them give you long speeches. Because you have that falsetto, and you have a couple of inches of area for inflection, and it'd be terrible to have a long speech in a falsetto voice."

Producer Harry Tytle said:

> Jimmy, while certainly talented, and who performed the voice well, was primarily called upon because he was already on salary, and his voice didn't add to the film's cost.

MacDonald remembered:

> One day I was doing something and Walt came on the dialog stage. As he turned to leave, he turned around to the fellow at the soundboard and said, "Hey, don't forget I do Mickey's voice, too."

However, MacDonald always felt his main job was running the sound-effects department. At the age of 82, he performed on *Late Night with David Letterman*, recalling:

> I had the best Mickey Mouse voice I'd had in a long time. It must have been the raw oysters I ate before I went on air.

Mickey's Voice: Wayne Allwine

Just a few months before Walt Disney died in 1966, twenty-year- old Wayne Allwine was hired for a job in the mail room at the Disney studio. From there, he worked in a variety of roles and eventually began a seven-and-a-half-year apprenticeship under Jimmy MacDonald, where he won awards for his sound-effects editing.

Allwine recalled:

> Jimmy decided to retire from doing Mickey's voice in 1976 so they began auditioning. Somebody missed their audition appointment. So they called the department where I worked and said, "Send the kid down if it's okay. We have a space here, and we want to put a name on the list." I'd never done anything like that before and didn't expect to ever do it again. A couple of months later, Disney executive Lou Debney stopped me on Mickey Avenue on the studio lot and said, "You've got to join the Screen Actors Guild, kid. They're going to use you."

Allwine made his Mickey vocal debut on *The New Mickey Mouse Club* (1977–1978), and provided Mickey's voice for Disney theme parks, movies, television specials, records, and video games for over three decades.

His premiere theatrical vocal appearance as Mickey Mouse was in *Mickey's Christmas Carol* (1983), the first new Mickey Mouse animated cartoon released to movie theaters in thirty years.

Over the years, Allwine continued to expand Mickey's dramatic repertoire by singing in *The Prince and the Pauper* (1990) and performing as an enormous monster in *Runaway Brain* (1995).

He was heard constantly as Mickey in everything from new cartoon shorts for the television series *Mickey Mouse Works* (1999) and *Disney's House of Mouse* (2001) to popular video games like the *Kingdom Hearts* series that began in 2002.

Wayne Allwine died on May 18, 2009. The last Disney product to feature his voice work, *Kingdom Hearts 358/2 Days*, has a dedication to his memory.

Allwine said:

> Mickey is an actor and he's capable of doing whatever he's given to do—provided it's kept in context of what Mickey would and wouldn't do. Walt always has been very much alive in Mickey Mouse and we try to direct him more toward Walt's version of Mickey who was an actor, forever young and forever optimistic.
>
> Jimmy [MacDonald] said to me, "Just remember, kid, you're only filling in for the boss." Mickey's the star. I get to take this wonderful American icon and keep it alive until the next Mickey comes along.

Mickey Imposter: Filthy Mickey

In order to protect its products, Disney is often placed in the position of aggressively enforcing its copyrights and trademarks, especially when the theft of the property might tarnish its brand. A facet of intellectual property law, called acquiescence, compels Disney to fight every infringement they find or give up the right to defend the trademark or copyright when it really matters.

MAD magazine began parodying specifically Mickey Mouse in issue #19 (January 1955) with the story "Mickey Rodent!" that lampoons the absurdity of the logic in the Disney cartooniverse. Artist Bill Elder aped the standard house artistic style of Disney and even added the "Walt Dizzy" signature at the bottom of the pages. However, writer Harvey Kurtzman's short story was a one-time use and obviously protected by the "fair use" right to parody.

National Lampoon magazine (Sept. 1970, Vol. 1, No. 6) had a cover with a cartoon of Minnie Mouse flashing so that she appears topless but with little yellow flower pasties on her nipples.

This cover was the brain-child of publisher Matty Simmons who wanted to bring attention to the struggling magazine and secretly hoped to spark Disney's ire and get the resulting publicity. Disney sued for $11 million, but it was settled out of court since it could be argued that a one-time use might be considered parody, especially considering the nature of this particular magazine.

In describing the Disneyland Memorial Orgy poster, *Time* magazine's Richard Corliss wrote:

> In Wally Wood's lushly scabrous "Disneyland Memorial Orgy," a 1967 parody that ran in *The Realist* magazine, Walt's creatures behaved exactly as barnyard and

woodland denizens might. Beneath dollar-sign searchlights radiating from the Magic Kingdom's castle, Goofy had his way with Minnie, Dumbo the flying elephant dumped on Donald Duck, the Seven Dwarfs besmirched Snow White en masse, and Tinker Bell performed a striptease for Peter Pan and Jiminy Cricket. Mickey slouched off to one side, shooting heroin.

Paul Krassner, the editor of *The Realist*, had contacted artist Wally Wood who had drawn Disney parodies in *MAD* magazine to create the blasphemous center spread for the satricial newpaper.

When an entrepreneur named Sam Ridge pirated the drawing and sold it as a black-light poster, Disney took legal action. The blatantly commercial nature of the bootleg and the fact that it would reach a much larger audience than the poorly distributed *The Realist* resulted in an out-of-court settlement forcing Ridge out of business.

Talking Mickey: Walt on the Mickey Audience

"To be honest about the matter, when our gang goes into a huddle and comes out with a new Mickey Mouse story, we will not have worried one bit as to whether the picture will make the children better men and women, or whether it will conform with the enlightened theories of child psychology. By laughing at Mickey's antics, youngsters learn to laugh at their own troubles. The period of their lives when they can live in a world peopled by fairy tale characters is all too short.

"It is not our job to teach, implant morals, or improve anything except our pictures. If Mickey has a bit of practical philosophy to offer the younger generation, it is to keep on trying. It is our hope and ambition to keep on trying so that these children will have the Mickey in them released and nourished by better cartoons than we make today.

"The Mickey audience...it has no racial, national, political, religious, or social differences or affiliations. The Mickey audience is made up of parts of people, of that deathless, precious, ageless absolutely primitive remnant of something, in a very world-wracked human being that makes us play with children's toys and laugh without self-consciousness at silly things and sing in bathtubs, and dream. You know...the Mickey in us.

"Ever since I first drew him, he has become more and more real, and like a real child. He is very real to me and to those fellow-workers of mine who guide his impish footsteps on the screen. We never think of him as a mouse. Nor as a drawing. He is always human.

"When we are first discussing the script of a new picture, we actually go through the scene ourselves. It is just as if we are planning scenes for a living star. Mickey's a very busy young star—and the only one in Hollywood who isn't paid! I often regret that it is impossible to reward him in some way for all the fun he has given to the world.

"Mickey's been my passport to everything I've wanted to do. When I felt I should branch out a little.... I wanted to try pure beauty in cartoons. I wanted to try animating great music. I had a lot of ideas—but all the exhibitors wanted was Mickey. Okay, I gave them Mickey, but they had to take my Silly Symphonies, too, in order to get him."

Jungle Mickey

Jungle Rhythm (1929) had Mickey for the first time venturing into the African jungle where his gun falls apart so he has to use music to soothe the savage beasts. The Disney Channel once banned this cartoon from being shown under the assumption it had cannibal caricatures. It does not.

However, stereotyped versions of black cannibals do appear in Mickey cartoons like *Trader Mickey* (1932) and *Mickey's Man Friday* (1935). Mickey had jungle adventures in his comic strip where he faced cannibals as well. In February 1930, Walt Disney wrote and Ub Iwerks drew the "Lost on a Desert Island" story continuity. In August 1932, Floyd Gottfredson had Mickey confront cannibals in "Mickey Mouse Sails for Treasure Island." Even the comic book *Dell Four Color* #181 had Mickey and Goofy in a full-length story called "Jungle Magic" in 1948.

Mickey also had some real-life jungle encounters:

A witch doctor in the Belgian Congo reportedly used a homemade mask of "Mikimus" to provide a little extra magic. When actor Douglas Fairbanks Sr. went on a world tour, he showed Mickey Mouse movies to headhunters of the South Seas islands to keep them friendly. In the 1930s, Kaffirs, members of a South African tribe, refused to take cakes of soap unless they were embossed with a Mickey Mouse image.

Disney costume designer Alice Davis told me:

> When [my husband, Disney artist and animator] Marc and I went to New Guinea in 1978, we were taken by a guide to a remote village in the rainforest that had had almost no contact with the outside world and had never seen a white person like us. As we stood there, this little child came running out of the forest wearing nothing except a Mickey Mouse t-shirt. Somehow, Mickey had made it there before anyone else.

Imagineer John Hench said:

> The attraction to Mickey is instinctual. Kids who scream bloody murder when their parents put them on Santa's lap will run up to Mickey and wrap their arms around his legs. In 1957, Dr. Tom Dooley of MEDICO [Medical International Cooperation Organization] put Mickey's face on the side of his hospital ship anchored off a southeastern Asian coast where even a Red Cross sign had no effect. It succeeded in luring children aboard for free examinations and treatment, even though hardly any of them had ever seen a picture of Mickey before. They just sensed it was safe and friendly.

Mickey Mouse 1935

- The first theatrical Technicolor Mickey Mouse cartoon short, *The Band Concert*, was released February 1935. The film won the Venice Film Festival Golden Medal for Best Animation. Italian conductor Arturo Toscanini saw it multiple times and invited Walt Disney to his home in Italy to discuss it. Over 468 million tickets were sold to Mickey Mouse cartoons in 1935.

- A 1935 *Time* magazine article stated: "Anyway, a current survey shows that children don't think of Mickey as a mouse. A good many of them were asked whether Mickey Mouse is a dog or a cat. Almost half of the tots answered brightly, 'A cat.'" Even though Mickey's last name is "Mouse."

- In 1935, against Disney's strict policy of not featuring Mickey on anything that would be distasteful to children, Walt allowed Mickey Mouse to promote Scott's Emulsion, a cod liver oil, but only in South America because of the high incidence of rickets there.

- Worcester, Massachusetts, officially proclaimed May 12, 1935, as Mickey Mouse Day. A Mickey Mouse Mall was set up in front of City Hall. School children, the mayor, and the city council paid homage; restaurants had Mickey Mouse on their tablecloths; clerks had Mickey Mouse on their smocks; and the *Boston Herald* began its lead editorial: "They are making history today in Worchester. They also made money."

- In 1935, it was reported that the favorite toys of the famous Dionne quintuplets of Canada were their Mickey Mouse rattles.

- In 1935, Romanian authorities banned Mickey Mouse films from cinemas after they feared that children would be "scared to see a ten-foot mouse in the movie theatre."

- In 1935, one-third of the population of the small town of Norwich, New York, were earning enough money from overtime just from making Mickey Mouse sweatshirts to support their families. That year, over one million Mickey Mouse sweatshirts were sold.

- The first issue of the newsstand *Mickey Mouse Magazine* appeared on May 15, 1935, and sold nearly 150,000 copies. It lasted until September 1940 when it was converted into a comic book, *Walt Disney's Comics and Stories*.

- The slogan for *Mickey Mouse Magazine* was "A Fun Book for Children to Read to Grown-ups." Roy O. Disney told publisher Hal Horne that the slogan was accurate because his young son [Roy E. Disney] spent an entire evening at a polo match reading the first issue and pestering his father by reading him the jokes.

- In 1935, Sam Buchwald, part of the management team of Fleischer Studios who were producing Betty Boop and Popeye short cartoons, told writer Bosley Crowther of the New York Times newspaper: "Familiar cartoon characters rise, have their day of great popularity, and then wane just as real stars do. Although Disney doesn't say much about it, his lovable Mickey, greatest animated character of all time, is definitely on the way out. And where are Koko the Clown, Mutt and Jeff, and other of those favorites of a bygone era?"

Why Did Mickey Mouse's Eyes Change?

Animator Frank Thomas said:
> Mickey's eyes were a special problem. They had started as black pupils in large eyes that looked more like googles than an eye shape. Since the whole figure was stock cartoon formula for the time, the eyes worked well.

The rims of Mickey's eyes gradually got so large that they seemed to resemble eyebrows with two mirrored curved lines near the top of the head. The pupil of his eye also got bigger and was considered by the audience Mickey's actual eye, very much like a solid black eye on a doll.

While this image was appealing, it became almost impossible to draw Mickey looking in any direction other than directly in front of his face. Mickey's head had to be raised to make him look up or turned to look to the side.

Especially for Mickey's appearances in print, including film posters, it was necessary for a viewer to be able to tell where Mickey was looking. The solution was the "pie-eye." The name referred to the fact that a black oval eye would have a triangular section, much like a slice being removed from a whole pie, in white. This triangle supposedly represented a highlight from a light source that showed where Mickey was looking.

This technique was primarily used on print images and merchandising in the 1930s but also appeared in Mickey animated shorts beginning with *The Karnival Kid* (1929).

The first use of the now-familiar eyes in the white area of Mickey Mouse's face was an illustration done by animator Ward Kimball for the cover of a Disney party program held on June 4, 1938. He felt it gave Mickey more personality. Some at the studio, including animator Fred Moore and Walt himself, liked it.

Disney animator Ollie Johnston said:

> When some animators were pressuring Walt to let them change Mickey's eyes so that more delicate expressions could be handled, Walt asked Don [Graham, Chouinard art instructor teaching at the Disney studio] to bring it up in his class to see what all of the fellows thought.
>
> It was a difficult night for Don [as he] found himself trying to control a spirited discussion between authorities of varied opinions and even more varied personalities. Some felt the audience would never accept the new design and would wonder what was wrong. Others claimed that people would never notice. Some felt it would be all right to try it for just one picture and see what happened.
>
> As the talk became more heated, one man [animator Bill Tytla] quipped, "Why don't we just change one eye at a time?"

It was finally decided that it was the time to make the change. *Society Dog Show* (1939) was the last short to feature Mickey's "dot" eyes.

Officially, *The Pointer* (1939) was the first short released with Mickey having his now-familiar pupils. When it started production, the original model sheets had Mickey with the older-style eyes, but that was changed.

However, released months earlier for both the 1939 New York's World Fair and the San Francisco Golden Gate International Exposition was a commercial short entitled *Mickey's Surprise Party* for the Nabisco company and it featured Mickey with the new eyes.

Mickey Mouse comic strip artist Floyd Gottfredson said:

> When I first saw the pupils in Mickey's eyes in model sheets in 1938, I liked it immediately although it was hard for me to do for a while until I got used to it.

With the release of *Fantasia* (1940), Mickey's new eyes became the accepted standard and audiences had no difficulty accepting them.

Where Do the Stories Come From? 'The Castaway' (1931)

In *The Castaway,* Mickey is washed ashore on a tropical island along with a piano that he uses to entertain the animals. He has misadventures with a gorilla, a lion, and a crocodile, and later escapes the island on the back of a tortoise. It's the first Disney cartoon featuring music by composer Frank Churchill.

Director Wilfred Jackson recalled:

> Walt was behind on schedule and needed something to catch up with and he had a lot of footage that had been cut out of other cartoons [*Jungle Rhythm* and *Wild Waves*] and it was saved in the morgue. All the animation was done and my first job was to make some kind of a story where we could use all this discarded stuff.
>
> The only way I could see to tie all this stuff together was to have Mickey be cast away on an island after his ship was wrecked and to be sort of a Robinson Crusoe character and had all kinds of materials that had come from the ship, including a piano, and all the things that were needed for all the different scenes and it would be on an island where there are jungle creatures to use gags about jungle animals from the various cut footage.

Mickey's First Books

- The first Mickey Mouse book, published in 1930 by Bibo and Lang, was just called *Mickey Mouse Book* and was more a magazine than a book. It was fifteen pages long with a game and game board as well as a marching song. The main four-page story of how Mickey was kicked out of Mouse Fairyland and then met Walt Disney who made him a star was written by Bobette Bibo, the eleven-year-old daughter of one of the publishers. Roughly 100,000 copies were printed and sold over a six-month span. It sold for fifteen cents.

- The first Mickey Mouse coloring book was produced by the Saalfield Publishing Company of Ohio in 1931. It was an oversized eleven inches by fifteen inches book of thirty pages of drawings and short captions. Some of the drawings were partially colored to aid young artists on appropriate colors to use. Saalfield was also responsible for the first Mickey and Minnie paper doll book.

- Whitman Publishing of Racine, Wisconsin, released its first ten Big Little Books in 1932 and Mickey was the star of one of them. Each book was four inches wide and four-and-a-half inches high and about one-and-a-half inches thick. On one page would be text and on the facing page would be a black-and-white illustration. They only cost a dime.

- Over two dozen different Mickey Mouse Big Little Books were published between 1932 and 1949. The very first Mickey Mouse Book released in 1932 comes in two different cover versions. The first has a crudely drawn Mickey and a Walt Disney signature on the cover while the second version has a more pleasing, standard Mickey without the signature. While the covers and back covers are different, they both retain the same number, #717, and interior design.

- Several Big Little Books published by Whitman Publishing were used as premiums. *Mickey Mouse, the Mail Pilot* was given away by the American Oil Company and Clark Drugstores. *Mickey Mouse Sails for Treasure Island* was a premium for Kolynos Dental Cream. Two special editions were produced for Santa at Macy's Department Store to hand out to children at the holiday season in the Toyland section of the store: *Mickey Mouse and Minnie at Macy's* (1934) and *Mickey Mouse and Minnie March to Macy's* (1935).

- The first issue of *Mickey Mouse Magazine* appeared on newsstands on May 15, 1935, and sold nearly 150,000 copies at a dime each (although that first issue sold for a quarter before the ten-cent price became the norm with the second issue when it became a monthly publication). It was typical of the standard children's magazines of the time, with a mixture of short stories, poems, puzzles, and drawings.

Men Behind the Mouse: Fred Moore

Robert Fred Moore, often referred to as "Freddy" or "Freddie," was an animator whose work is still studied today for his ability to get a sense of "appeal" in his characters. He was born September 7, 1911, and died November 23, 1952.

Moore is credited with the more appealing redesign of Mickey Mouse in the mid-1930s, including the pear-shaped body, cheeks, and the effective addition of pupils to Mickey's eyes.

When he first showed these changes to Walt in a "sweatbox" session where preliminary work was reviewed, Moore was nervous, especially knowing Walt's deep connection to Mickey Mouse.

Walt re-ran the scene several times without saying a word. Then, Walt lifted his eyebrow, turned to Moore, and said, "Now that's the way I want Mickey to be drawn from now on!"

When he was hired at the Disney studio, Moore became an assistant to Les Clark, the Mickey Mouse specialist at the time, having been an assistant to Ub Iwerks. Soon, it was Moore who was considered the Mickey specialist.

In the late 1930s, sometime before 1938, Moore gave an illustrated presentation to the Disney animators about how to approach the character of Mickey Mouse. Entitled "Analysis of Mickey Mouse," it was part of a series of lectures given by top Disney animators like Art Babbit, Norm Ferguson, and Fred Spencer on the characters of Goofy, Pluto, and Donald Duck.

Moore said:

> Mickey seems to be the average young boy of no particular age; living in a small town, clean-living, fun-loving,

bashful around girls, polite and clever as he must be for the particular story. In some pictures he has a touch of Fred Astaire; in others of Charlie Chaplin, and some of Douglas Fairbanks, but in all of these there should be some of the young boy.

About the construction of the figure, he said:

The legs are better drawn tapering from the pant leg to the shoe, that is, larger at the shoe with the knee coming low on the leg. This also applies to the arms; the hands being fairly large.

And about handling Mickey in animation, he said:

The ears are better kept far back on the head and often act as a balance for the figure. However, do not shift them around on the head just to balance.

Mickey Imposter: Count Cutelli

In the U.K. *South Eastern Times* newspaper for Tuesday August 23, 1932, it states:

> Mickey Mouse, or rather his voice, arrived in London recently. He is Count Mazzaglia Cutelli, an Italian, who can produce from his throat more than 2,000 sound effects. Count Cutelli has been Mickey Mouse's screen voice ever since the count went to Hollywood.

Gaetano Mazzaglia dei Conti Cutelli was born in Italy and came to the United States in 1923. His repertoire of sounds included not just animals, but mechanical and weather effects. Cutelli did work for cartoons produced by Leon Schlesinger at Warner Bros. as well as the croaking of a bullfrog in a Disney cartoon.

The November 1932 Decca records catalogue supplement lists a 10-inch blue label record titled MICKEY MOUSE DISCOVERS A NEW LAND backed with MICKEY MOUSE ON THE ISLAND OF THE POLAR BEARS [by] Count Mazzaglia Cutelli of Mickey Mouse Fame (Novelty Cartoon Record)." It was listed as Record No. F3175.

The description states

> At last the effects side of the Mickey Mouse cartoons has been recorded by the originator of the effects, Count Cutelli. Indeed this unique record should have universal appeal, irrespective of age and class. It should be stated that all effects are devised and performed by Count Cutelli, and they are exactly as they appear in the series of talking films under the general title of Mickey Mouse.

However, later editions of that same catalogue included the following notice:

> This record has been withdrawn as it has come to the notice of the Decca Record Co. Ltd. that Count Mazzaglia Cutelli is not connected with and has no authority from

Mr. Walter Disney the originator of Mickey Mouse to use the name of Mickey Mouse or make any record purporting to reproduce the sound effects employed in the Mickey Mouse pictures. The Decca Record Co. Ltd. begs to announce that at the request of Mr. Disney all copies of this record have been destroyed and takes this opportunity of expressing to users of Decca Records the company's regret that this record should ever have been issued as representing or reproducing the sound effects of the Mickey Mouse cartoons.

Cutelli, if he is remembered at all, will receive recognition for the installation of his sound-effects equipment (personally installed by him) in radio stations and motion picture studios throughout Europe and the United States.

Mickey Cartoons: 'Hollywood Party'

Hollywood Party (1934) was planned as a lavish, star-studded MGM musical revue, but the production dragged on seemingly forever and used the talents of five directors (none of whom were credited) and seven writers who all tried to make some sense of the material.

The originally announced "all-star" cast slowly dwindled down to inexpensive contract players Jimmy Durante and Jack Pearl (radio's Baron Munchhausen) and a parade of celebrity cameos sometimes of non-MGM personalities.

The final film told an odd story about the Great Schnarzan (Durante), a jungle-movie star like Tarzan, who throws a huge Hollywood party in a convoluted plan to purchase some healthy lions to bring some much-needed zip to his films.

The party is just an excuse to showcase short comedy bits from everyone from Laurel and Hardy to the Three Stooges to Mickey Mouse.

In September 1933, a contract was drawn up for the Disney studio to produce a segment in black and white for the film where Mickey Mouse would crash the party and engage in some interplay with the main star of the film, comedian Durante who often made fun of his huge nose.

While the sequence was only supposed to be 75 feet of footage, it ended up nearly twice that length at roughly 132 feet.

One of the challenges was that the MGM writers didn't understand how to write for Mickey, primarily a visual character who spoke in short phrases.

When Mickey disrupts the party, the writers had him saying, "Now that the tumult has subsided," a phrase that was very un-Mickey.

There were several suggested actions for Mickey including having him enter the party by skipping among the glasses of drinks that have been left on the bar and reaching into a martini glass and taking out an olive to munch.

Finally, a script was devised (credited to Ned Marin) where women scream that a mouse is loose at the party and Jimmy Durante picks up the rodent from the floor by its tail to discover that it is Mickey Mouse. Mickey stretches out his snout and does an imitation of Durante then has some good-natured banter with the star.

It is the first time that an animated Mickey interacts with a live performer on the silver screen.

Then, at Durante's urging, Mickey sits at a cartoon piano and begins to play the music for *Hot Chocolate Soldiers* that fades into a short Technicolor cartoon of the same name also produced for the film by the Disney studio. (The rest of the film, including the Mickey Mouse segment, is in black and white.)

Most of the production work for the Mickey Mouse scene was done in October, with the final footage delivered to MGM on November 8, 1933.

Disney historian J.B. Kaufman discovered that "the Disney exposure sheets suggest that the Mouse animation was largely in the hands of Fred Moore."

The completed film was released in June 1934 and to show how important Mickey Mouse was at the time, he receives his own separate title card in the credits just like the big name live-action actors. One film reviewer of the time claimed that the Disney animation was the only bright spot in the entire film.

Because of the contract, the Disney sequences from the film were removed when the film was released to television in 1957. That's the way the film was shown for more than three decades until the Disney scenes were restored for the 1992 video edition released after some negotiation with the Disney company.

Minnie Moments

PRINCESS MINNIE: Minnie portrayed a princess in the cartoon shorts *Ye Olden Days* (1933) and *Brave Little Tailor* (1938). In *Mickey, Donald, Goofy: The Three Musketeers* (2004) she is the princess of France. Mickey once said, "Gosh, Minnie, you've always been a princess to me."

Princess Minnie was to appear in a September 1939 proposed but never made Mickey Mouse short cartoon entitled "Mickey's Swing Band." Leigh Harline and Ned Washington composed a song called "Minnie, the Princess." The storyline was that Minnie is a sheltered and highly cultured princess but very lonely. One day she hears a record of *Mickey Hot-Stuff and His Band* and loses interest in classical music. She refuses to be crowned queen until Mickey is brought to the palace and made her king.

NO KISSING: Mickey and Minnie kissing in the 1930s sparked letters from concerned parents that it was undermining the morality of youth. Director Federico Fellini told film critic Roger Ebert, "I love it when Mickey and Minnie kiss and the little hearts pop around them."

THANK HEAVEN FOR MINNIE: In *Mickey's Nightmare* (1932), Mickey kneels by his bed before going to sleep and says, "God bless Minnie, God Bless Pluto, God bless everyone."

NICE NIECES: In American comic books, artist Paul Murry introduced Minnie's twin nieces Melody and Millie. He later called them Pammy and Tammy when he used them again because he may have forgotten they had been already named. In other American comic books, Minnie has a single niece named Molly. In European and Brazilian comics, Minnie has a single niece named Melody, the creation of Jim Fletcher in the mid-1960s. Mickey's single niece Maisie appears only in the cartoon *Gulliver Mickey* (1934).

Talking Mickey: Walt on Mickey's Appearance

"I wanted something appealing, something wistful; a grand little fellow trying to do the best he could. Mickey appeared before my eyes. What could be more wistful, more cute, more appealing than a little mouse?

"Mickey had to be simple. We had to push out seven hundred feet of film every two weeks so we couldn't have a character who was tough to draw. We evolved him out of circles. They were simple and easy to handle. His head was a circle with an oblong circle for a snout. The ears were also circles so they could be drawn the same, no matter how he turned his head.

"His body was like a pear and he had a long tail. His legs were pipe stems and we stuck them in big shoes. We didn't want him to have mouse hands, because he was supposed to be more human. So we gave him gloves.

"Five fingers seemed like too much on such a little figure, so we took away one. That was just one less finger to animate. Leaving the finger off was a great asset artistically and financially. That missing digit saves us at least several thousand dollars a year in artists' time.

"To provide a little detail, we gave him the two-button pants. There was no mouse hair or any other frills that would slow down animation. That made it tougher for the cartoonists to give him character. When people laugh at Mickey, it's because of his humanity and that is the secret of his popularity.

"And it is certainly gratifying that the public which first welcomed him as well as their children have not permitted us, even if we had wished, to change him in any manner or degree, other than a few minor revisions of his physical appearance. In a sense he was never young.

In the same sense, he never grows old in our eyes. All we can do is give him things to overcome in his own, rather stubborn way, in his cartoon universe.

"He's a little better-constructed mouse than he ever was. He's improved with age. After all, you can't expect charm from animated sticks and that is what Mickey Mouse was in his first pictures.

"All we planned or expected was that the audience everywhere would laugh with him or at him for pleasure. As long as there's a Disney studio, there'll be Mickey Mouse cartoons. I can't live without them."

Hidden Mickey

A "hidden Mickey" is an image of Mickey Mouse "hidden" at a Disney venue like a theme park, a restaurant, or a cruise ship. Usually, it is the tri-circled silhouette of Mickey's head that might be found in a swirl on a piece of furniture or an arrangement of rocks and plants or a carpet pattern or some other grouping in a context that might not normally contain Mickey.

Some hidden Mickeys are much cleverer, like Mickey's foot on a 1930s movie poster peeking out beneath the *Public Enemy* movie poster in the gangster scene of the Great Movie Ride for over two decades at Disney Hollywood Studios. Like many hidden Mickeys, it no longer exists.

One of the first unofficial Hidden Mickeys was in the 1955 Disneyland Rocket to the Moon attraction where the rapidly diminishing spaceport (designed by Imagineer John Hench) in the bottom viewport resembled Mickey's head.

The current unofficial hidden Mickeys originated at Epcot Center in 1982. The secret was revealed to the general public in the December 1991 issue of *Disney News* magazine in an article by Imagineer David Fisher:

> When EPCOT Center opened at Walt Disney World in 1982, a conscious decision was made to give the new Theme Park a distinctly separate identity from the older, more familiar Magic Kingdom. One of the ways this was done was to purposely keep all references to the Disney characters out of the new Park.
>
> Leave it to the devious denizens of Walt Disney Imagineering to work the familiar ears or silhouette into just about anything they could during those early, no-Mouse days of EPCOT Center.
>
> Tributes to Mickey Mouse do not begin and end in EPCOT Center. Disney's forever-fresh-faced star is hidden in many places around Walt Disney World.

Actually, Disney cast members had been alerted to the practice two years earlier by fellow cast members Arlen Miller and Bob Weir in their "Hidden Disney" article for the November 30, 1989, edition of the cast member newspaper *Eyes and Ears* (Vol. 19, No 48).

Miller told me:

> I had some WDI friends who would sometimes mention the Hidden Mickey in some of the attractions, but no one was supposed to know about it.
>
> Then one day I thought I would try to find them. I found all of them in Epcot and the Studios and decided to write about it with a co-writer. When they [*Eyes and Ears*] got our article the editor had never heard of this before, so he phoned Imagineering to confirm it. By chance, he got connected directly to [executive vice president of Imagineering] Marty Sklar. He read him the article over the phone and Marty acknowledged each of the examples we mentioned in the article.
>
> Finally, he asked how we knew about this stuff since it was supposed to be an Imagineering secret. He graciously gave a statement for print that said, "This is just one more reward for the true Disney fan—discovering these hidden details. It's also part of the magic of creating the fun—you've got to have fun doing it, too." I then heard from the *Disney News* magazine several months later and they interviewed me on the phone about it for 45 minutes.

There is no official, complete listing of hidden Mickeys since they were done in an impromptu fashion and areas are constantly changing. Some Mickey images are intentionally included in a design and are considered "decorative Mickeys".

Some Imagineers prefer not to encourage the guests' fascination with the phenomenon because they feel it distracts guests from being immersed in the entire experience.

Hidden Mickeys You May Have Missed

UNDER THE SEA: JOURNEY OF THE LITTLE MERMAID (Walt Disney World): The rarest Hidden Mickey can only be seen on November 18, Mickey's birthday, at noon if the sun is shining. Imagineers drilled three holes in the ceiling that on that day and time will create the famous three-circle Mickey image on the wall of the queue line at about knee-level. It has appeared for just a few minutes every year since the attraction was first opened in 2012.

BUZZ LIGHTYEAR'S SPACE RANGER SPIN (Walt Disney World): In the queue line guests can spot several references to the planet Pollust Prime which features a continent in the center that forms a sideways Hidden Mickey in silhouette. At Disneyland in Buzz Lightyear Astro Blasters, it is hidden in the murals of the Ska-densii planets.

PETER PAN'S FLIGHT (Disneyland): A profile of Mickey is in one of the windows as you move around the back of the Big Ben clock tower.

MICKEY'S TOONTOWN HOUSE (Disneyland): Several books on the shelves have a variety of different Mickey images on their spines.

THE LITTLE MERMAID (1989): At the start of the film, during King Triton's entrance into the concert theater with his trident held high as he rides in his turtle shell chariot pulled by dolphins, to the lower left are full figures of Goofy, Donald Duck, and Mickey facing toward the stage. Another guest to the lower right in the same frame is wearing a Mickey Mouse ears hat.

TRON (1982): At the end of the film, Flynn and Yori escape aboard a "solar sailer simulation" and travel through an open plain that reveals a large hidden Mickey facing sideways underneath their ship.

The Rescuers (1977): In the beginning, when the Rescue Aid Society assembles beneath the United Nations in New York City, the clock on the wall is actually a Mickey Mouse wrist watch.

Aladdin (1992): After Jafar is defeated, the baby tiger cub Rajah's face as he is being held by the sultan briefly morphs into Mickey Mouse's face before returning to normal.

Wreck-It Ralph (2012): Mickey Mouse is on a Double U Dee's billboard behind and above Litwak's Arcade just to the right side at the very beginning of the film.

How to Be a Detective (1952): Mickey's face is on the front cover of the comic book Goofy is reading.

Fantasmic!

Fantasmic! is a complex nighttime entertainment show mixing water effects, fireworks, film, music, and dozens of live performers at Disneyland, Walt Disney World, and Tokyo Disneyland. All three versions have significant differences, though the basic story premise remains the same with Mickey doing battle with the classic Disney villains who have invaded his imagination.

The origin of the show goes back to September 1990 when Robert McTyre, vice president of Disneyland Entertainment, got a phone call from CEO Michael Eisner.

McTyre recalled:

> [Eisner] said, "We don't have anything big and new and fabulous for Disneyland in 1992 and we need to come up with something." Basically, it was an interim step to keep interest in Disneyland high before the 1993 addition of Mickey's Toontown.

Original director Barnette Ricci said:

> We were asked to create something spectacular for Disney using the Rivers of America. We wanted something truly unique that combined a lot of spectacular effects that people hadn't seen before and with a story about Mickey Mouse that would really involve people.
>
> The core for the show was the water screens. It would be unique to project Disney animation onto one of those screens. Mickey Mouse's imagination creates these images and the audience gets involved with Mickey.

Originally, the show was going to be called "Imagination," but the Disney company found it could not copyright that title so once again created a uniquely Disney-esque word. The opening narration sets the story for the show:

> Welcome to Fantasmic! Tonight, our friend and host Mickey Mouse uses his vivid imagination to create magical imagery for all to enjoy. Nothing is more

wonderful than the imagination. For, in a moment, you can experience a beautiful fantasy. Or, an exciting adventure!

But beware—nothing is more powerful than the imagination. For it can also expand your greatest fears into an overwhelming nightmare. Are the powers of Mickey's incredible imagination strong enough, and bright enough, to withstand the evil forces that invade Mickey's dreams?

Near the end of the performance, Mickey transforms into his Sorcerer Mickey persona and defeats the Disney villains who have troubled his peaceful animated dreams including the evil Maleficent who transforms herself into a massive fire-breathing dragon. For the Walt Disney World version the finale includes Mickey as Steamboat Willie piloting a steamboat filled with Disney costumed characters.

Mickey Cartoons: 'The Talking Dog'

Around 1996, specialist Scott MacQueen, who spent twelve years at the Disney company preserving and restoring films, uncovered the scratch track (the preliminary rough voice and sound-effects track) and some completed animation for a 1951 Mickey Mouse cartoon that was abandoned called *The Talking Dog*.

Fred Moore did the Mickey animation, and the Pluto animation was done by Norm Ferguson. Milt Schaffer directed.

Pluto has been a bad dog messing up the house and a stern Mickey Mouse exiles him outside. As a sad Pluto walks along the side of the road, he is scooped up by Black Pete in what looks like a moving van with the lettering "Miracle Medicine Show."

Pete's concoction is "the medicine that takes warts off frogs, turns hiccups into teacups and guaranteed to cure the Texas tickle!"

The tricky medicine man decides to entice customers to buy his wares by convincing them that Pluto can speak. Using his ventriloquist skill, he asks Pluto how he feels, and the poor pup seems to answer: "Just like a piano... GRAND!"

Of course, to perform this "miracle," Pluto must drink the horrible medicine first that makes him sick. Pluto soon gets tired of this sideshow career and longs to return home.

When Mickey can't find his beloved pet, he goes on a search that ends with a struggle with Pete on top of the careening truck as Pluto steers with his teeth. At one point, as they approach a covered bridge, they both leap from the top of the truck to the bridge and continue battling across it until they jump back onto the top of the van as it exits the bridge. The driverless van smashes into a huge tree and Mickey recovers Pluto.

Mickey asks Pluto if he is okay, and Pluto responds, "Grand! Grand!"

Disney producer Harry Tytle claimed that the short in its rough form got a low rating when it was screened for the other animators:

> I had thought *Talking Dog* was a weak story. Too much dialog and we didn't have the animators capable of doing a good job. At the time we first viewed the rough animation, I told Walt it was so bad that I called everyone concerned into a meeting. Three hundred feet of changes, new animation, went into the picture. The basic change was to make it a Pluto story, but the animation by Ferguson was bad.

Mickey At Sea

Mickey Mouse is more than just the captain of the ships on the Disney Cruise Line and on the official logo. He is everywhere, from an upper deck children's pool shaped like Mickey's face to the Golden Mickeys stage show mimicking the Oscar ceremony with golden Mickey statuettes to hidden Mickeys in the rope design of the shower curtains and the scroll work around the midship elevators.

Guests can even help Mickey solve a pair of mysteries as part of the Midship Detective Agency run by the Mouse.

All of the Disney cruise ships are painted in colors that match the famous mouse—white structure, black hull, two big red funnels, and the special yellow of Mickey's shoes for the lifeboats that required special permission from the International Maritime Organization to use.

Throughout the ship there is not only artwork from some of Mickey's nautical adventures like *Boat Builders* (1938), there is even a photo of Walt Disney holding a Mickey Mouse doll and strolling with his wife along the deck of the Italian luxury ship, *The Rex*, on a 1934 vacation. Exclusive DCL merchandise is available that features Mickey Mouse in his captain's uniform as well as frequent meet-and-greet opportunities with the costumed character.

Hidden underwater in the snorkeling lagoon at Castaway Cay is a statue of a ship's figurehead Mickey located to the left side near the wreckage around buoy B.

On the *Disney Magic*, the "Helmsman Mickey" bronze statue in the midship atrium on Deck 3 was designed by Imagineer John Hench. Hench was inspired by Leonard Craske's famous eight-foot tall 1923 (the year the Disney studio began) statue *Man at the Wheel*, showcased at the Fisherman's Memorial in Gloucester, Massachusetts. Like the original, it serves as a monument to the bravery and dedication of sailors everywhere. There is an exact copy of the statue at Tokyo DisneySea in Japan.

Sorcerer Mickey is displayed on the bow of the *Disney Magic* and *Disney Fantasy*; the bow of the *Disney Wonder* has Steamboat Willie and the bow of the *Disney Dream* is Captain Mickey. The three-dimensional Sorcerer Mickey Mouse on the *Disney Dream*'s stern is about 14 feet long. It was constructed out of stainless steel and fiberglass and weighs approximately 2,500 pounds.

Mickey will be equally prominent in the three currently unnamed new DCL ships that will launch beginning in 2021.

Mickey Cartoons: 'From Mouse to Duck'

In an interview in a 1949 issue of *Collier's* magazine, Walt Disney stated:

> Mickey's decline was due to his heroic nature. He grew into such a legend that we couldn't gag around with him. He acquired as many taboos as a Western hero—no smoking, no drinking, no violence.

Jimmy MacDonald, who provided the voice for Mickey for almost four decades, recalled:

> I remember when Walt was in a story meeting one time and they were showing him the storyboards and reading the dialog. He was smiling and everybody thought, 'Oh, this is great.' If Walt was smiling, then it was going over well. But when he was through, he said, "No, we're not going to make it." And they couldn't understand why. Then he said, "I don't want Mickey put into those situations."

Animator and director Jack Hannah stated:

> I remember many stories were started with Mickey, but as soon as they started to rough the Mouse up, Walt would come up and say, "Well, that's more of a Donald Duck story," so they'd turn around and make it a Donald Duck story.

One classic example of a Mickey story being transformed into a Donald story was *Yukon Mickey*, a 1930s unproduced short that was partially storyboarded with Mickey Mouse as a Canadian Mountie but was completely reboarded with Donald Duck in the part. Neither version was made.

In a story meeting on February 21, 1938, Walt Disney said:

> This picture might be suited better for the Duck as you would be able to use more personality with the Duck in spots than you would with Mickey. The expression and

the voice of the Duck would help it. It is a natural for the Duck to get in a situation like this—and the audience likes to see the Duck get it.

In 1948, he stated:

> It's tough to come up with new ideas for Mickey, to keep him fresh and at the same time in character. The Duck's a lot easier. You can do anything with him.
>
> I have always kind of compared Mickey to Harold Lloyd—he has to have situations or he isn't funny. I'd rather not make Mickey [films] if we don't get the right idea for him. These things with the Duck are always funny, but if you try to pull those with Mickey, it seems like someone trying to be funny.

Mickey Mouse Ears

The most popular Mickey Mouse theme park souvenir is the famous black skull cap/beanie with round ears that in recent years has spawned multiple variations including customizable ears.

The head gear was designed for the original Mickey Mouse Club television show by Disney storyman Roy O. Williams, "The Big Mooseketeer," who based them on a gag in an early Mickey Mouse cartoon, *The Karnival Kid* (1929), where Mickey tips his ears like a hat to Minnie Mouse, repeating the same gag from an Oswald the Lucky Rabbit cartoon *Sleigh Bells* (1928).

The man who actually made the first ones was Chuck Keehne who was working at the well-renowned Western Costume Company in Hollywood before he was hired in April 1955 by the Disney studio.

Mickey Mouse Club authority George Grant wrote:

> According to Chuck's daughter, Bill Walsh, Hal Adelquist, Roy Williams, and Chuck worked together on this. The early versions were too large and looked ungainly, nor would they stay on when the kids danced or moved quickly.
>
> Eventually Chuck and his team devised small hand-crafted caps with wire-reinforced felt ears and rubber-bands that fit under the chin to hold them on, each one tailored to an individual Mouseketeer.
>
> They were time-consuming to make, and were a far cry in quality from the caps eventually marketed to viewers and Disneyland visitors. Each cap contained $20 worth of high-quality felt, and cost an additional five dollars to make, a considerable sum in those days, especially when multiplied by two dozen Mouseketeers. The child performers were charged a fine of fifty dollars if they lost their ears.

The ears sold at Disneyland originally were made by the Benay-Albee Novelty Company of Maspeth, New York, and sold for sixty-nine cents each. They were made of felt with two plastic ears. At first, they had an "M" on the front, but Walt quickly changed it to just the famous image of Mickey's face encircled in red so the hat could be trademarked against imitations. In the red circle were the names "Disneyland" and "Mickey Mouse."

In the last decade, a plethora of different styles of mouse ears have been introduced in a variety of colors and images including ones that light up.

The only photo of Walt Disney wearing mouse ears appeared in the December 1, 1956, issue of the *Saturday Evening Post* when his grandson Christopher spontaneously put it on his head while photographer Gene Lester was snapping pictures.

The 23rd World Youth Day, a Catholic youth festival in July 2008, was held in Australia and was attended by 500,000 young people from 200 different countries. A delegation of Catholic school children from Orange County, California, presented Pope Benedict XVI with a pair of Mickey Mouse ears.

His name had been embroidered onto the cap just like the ones available at Disneyland. While the pope smiled when accepting the gift, he did not put them on in place of his ecclesiastical skullcap.

'Partners' Statue

Disney Imagineer Blaine Gibson sculpted what is known as the *Partners* statue that resides at the hub in both Disneyland and Walt Disney World. The statue features Walt Disney holding Mickey Mouse's hand.

There were several different compositions that were considered. One featured a young Mickey running ahead and pulling Walt along. It was rejected because it seemed awkward for Mickey to be dragging Walt forward.

Another featured Walt with the rolled-up blueprints of Epcot in his right hand and using them to point forward. Yet another had Walt with an opened-handed wave while in Mickey's hand was a small black globe of the world with two mouse ears.

The size for Mickey Mouse in proportion to Walt Disney was chosen based on a brief moment from the animated short *The Pointer* (1939).

Animator Frank Thomas recalled:

> When he recorded the voice [for Mickey], [Walt] couldn't help but feel like Mickey and he added all these little gestures that were spontaneous with him. At one point [where Mickey was talking to a huge bear], he put out his hand like this [to indicate that Mickey was about 3 feet tall]; it was the only time we knew how big Walt thought Mickey was.

Imagineer Marty Sklar remembered being amazed at seeing Gibson and Imagineer John Hench spending hours discussing just exactly how Walt's five-fingered hand should hold Mickey's four-fingered one.

It was finally decided to base it on the one time that an animated Mickey held the hand of a real person. In *Fantasia* (1940), Mickey shakes the hand of conductor Leopold Stokowski at the end of the "Sorcerer's Apprentice" sequence.

The *Partners* statue was unveiled at Disneyland on November 18, 1993.

At the unveiling, Gibson told the press:

> Many people asked me what Walt might be saying as he stood there with Mickey, and the expression I tried to capture was Walt saying to Mickey, "Look what we've accomplished together," because truly they were very much a team through it all.

In June 1995, another *Partners* statue was installed in the hub of the Magic Kingdom at Walt Disney World. Tokyo Disneyland has a *Partners* statue as does Disney Studios Paris and there's another in the courtyard of Team Disney in Burbank, California.

Gibson said in May 1992:

> I don't think of Mickey as a real mouse. When I sculpt Mickey, I think of him as a young boy.

Mickey's Girlfriend: Minnie Mouse

Minnie Mouse was created to be a springboard for story ideas, giving Mickey someone to strive to impress, to rescue from danger, to share musical moments with.

Her personality shared similarities with Walt's wife, Lillian. She was independent, stubborn, feminine, a little shy, faithful, and had a fiery temper. Lillian was there during story meetings for the earliest Mickey cartoons held in the Disney living room.

Architect John Cowles Jr., who designed some of the buildings at the Burbank Disney studio, buildings at Disneyland, and the layout for Walt's backyard railroad, the Carolwood Pacific, revealed that Minnie Mouse was named after his mother, Minnie Lee Cowles.

Mrs. Cowles was the wife of Dr. John Vance Cowles Sr. who had been the Disney family physician for years and was the chief investor in Walt's first animation studio, Laugh-o-grams.

On behalf of her husband, Minnie served as the treasurer for Walt's company and often brought homemade sandwiches to the starving young animators who did not have enough money to buy a meal. Walt even lived briefly with the Cowles family when he ran out of money.

Cowles Jr. said that Walt personally told his parents that the name "Minnie" was chosen as a loving tribute to his mother and Walt later repeated that claim to him several times over the years.

When the Social Security Administration began keeping track of baby names in 1880, Minnie was the fifth most popular name in the country. It remained a top ten name until 1892, when it began its decline in popularity until today when it is not even in the top one thousand names.

Like Mickey, Minnie only did squeaks and squawks provided by Walt himself. Her first words were "yoo hoo" in *The Karnival Kid* (1929). In 1930, Marcellite Garner from the ink-and-paint department began doing Minnie's dialog. Thelma Boardman took over from approximately 1940–1942 followed by Ruth Clifford from around 1942–1952. Russi Taylor became Minnie's official voice in 1986 and remains in that role today.

In the earliest cartoons, Minnie wears a pillbox hat with a single yellow daisy. It was fashionable for women to wear hats adorned with flowers, but being a Depression-era mouse, Minnie could only use a flower from her own garden. She first wore a bow, a big blue one, in the cartoon *Mickey's Surprise Party* (1939), a five-minute Technicolor commerical made for the Nabisco company to be shown at the 1939 World's Fair. The change in headgear also suggested her moving, like Mickey, from a rural environment to a more upscale urban one.

The bow didn't officially become the iconic red bow until the debut of the original television *Mickey Mouse Club* in 1955 where the female Mouseketeers wore a red ribbon bow on their mouse ear hats.

In fact, during the Great Depression, Minnie was so poor that she apparently only had one pair of panties. She had patched a tear in them herself with a square piece of cloth that was often visible because her dress was so short but was guaranteed to get a smile or a laugh from the audience.

Her oversized shoes were meant to suggest that she was a little girl wearing her mother's shoes to try to look older.

Disney animator Fred Moore's analysis of her in the 1930s for other artists to follow included:

> Minnie is drawn the same as Mickey, substituting a skirt and lace panties for his pants. Minnie seems cuter with the skirts high on her body showing a large expanse of her lace panties. To make Minnie as feminine as

possible, her mouth could be smaller than Mickey's and her eyelids and eyelashes could help very much.

Animator Frank Thomas recalled:

> We always drew Minnie with real broad, feminine gestures. Most of the time, she was modest, shy and girlish. I think Minnie reflected Walt's idea of what a girl ought to be.

In January 1932, writer Merrill De Maris and artist Floyd Gottfredson did a Mickey Mouse newspaper comic strip story where her Uncle Dudley refers to Minnie as "Minerva." Obviously, this wasn't approved by Walt and the name was never used officially again.

Minnie only appeared in about half of the classic Mickey Mouse cartoons. She was often replaced by Pluto or the duo of Donald Duck and Goofy.

She appeared in her first cartoon without Mickey in 1942, *Out of the Frying Pan Into the Firing Line*. This three-minute short was made for the conservation division of the War Production Board to illustrate the necessity of saving fats and greases that can be turned into glycerine for ammunition.

Her next appearance without Mickey was in the theatrical short *First Aiders* (1944) where Minnie practices her nursing skills on Figaro the cat and Pluto.

Men Behind the Mouse: Floyd Gottfredson

The Mickey Mouse comic strip debuted in January 13, 1930, with Walt doing the writing and Ub Iwerks pencilling them. After the first eighteen strips, Iwerks left and Win Smith took over the penciling and the inking, but he had a short fuse and quit when he was told to also do the writing. Gottfredson remembered:

> Walt came by my desk in April 1930 and said, "I think you've got a new job." I had told him I wanted to do comic strips when he hired me as an inbetweener.
>
> By now I had become very interested in animation and told Walt that I would prefer to stay with animation. Well, Walt was quite a salesman. He told me to just take the strip for two weeks to give him some time to find another artist.
>
> I wanted to help out so I agreed. I began enjoying doing it. Nothing more was ever said about it and I continued to draw the Mickey daily strip for about forty-five-and-a-half years until my retirement on October 1, 1975.
>
> I tried to follow the spirit of the Mickey animated cartoons, but because we were doing adventure stories we had to go beyond them. The animated cartoons had just a loose story structure where there could be a lot of gags building to a conclusion. That isn't how stories are done in newspaper strips. We had to develop the characters more to help sustain the story.
>
> Walt personally checked my work for the first couple of months after I took over the strip, but after that and all through the years, except to pass on an occasional suggestion, he very seldom concerned himself with the strip or the department. He seemed relieved not to have to be concerned with them. He had bigger things to worry about.
>
> Mostly, I tried to keep up with the changes the studio made to Mickey. I tried hard to match the Mickey I was drawing

for the newspaper strip with the Mickey of the films.

To me, the finest Mickey short cartoon that was ever made was *The Nifty Nineties* (1941) with Fred Moore's design of Mickey. I've said this many times before, but I think the best Mickeys ever done were by Fred Moore. I tried to imitate Fred, but I don't think anyone could ever copy his style. I was just doing the best I could as an extension of Walt and his dream.

Born May 5, 1905, Floyd Gottfredson was about twenty-four years old when he moved from his home in Utah with his wife and two children to Los Angeles in the hope of becoming a cartoonist for one of the seven major newspapers in the Hollywood-Los Angeles area. He had learned cartooning through a mail-order correspondence course.

Arriving in Los Angeles but finding no work in his field, he overheard that Walt Disney was looking for artists. He took his samples to the Disney studio and was immediately hired as an animation in-betweener and possible backup artist for the Mickey Mouse daily strip.

He started drawing the Mickey Mouse comic strip on May 5, 1930, and drew his last Sunday strip on September 19, 1976, and his last daily strip on November 15, 1976. Adding to his workload was a Mickey Mouse Sunday strip which Gottfredson penciled from January 10, 1932, until mid-1938, when Manuel Gonzales took over that strip.

Gottfredson said:

> I always felt that Mickey should have been a little [Charlie] Chaplin mouse against the world and I tried to promote that idea when they dropped the continuity and started the gag-a-day strips. Mickey had become bland and wishy-washy, too much like Dagwood and Blondie, in the neighborhood format. But my idea for changing Mickey's personality was rejected.
>
> I've always felt that it was our job to try to capture the spirit of animation. ... I tried to design the characters as if they were moving in animation.

Mickey Mouse Kills King Kong

In 1933, the same year *King Kong* was released and years before *Snow White and the Seven Dwarfs* (1937), Walt Disney was in discussion with *Kong*'s producer, Merian C. Cooper, about making a co-production Technicolor animated film of the popular Victor Herbert operetta *Babes in Toyland* for RKO.

Eventually, RKO did make a live-action black-and-white version of the operetta in 1934 featuring Laurel and Hardy with a live Mickey Mouse (a trained capuchin monkey dressed in a Mickey Mouse costume and mask who tormented the cat with the fiddle and later helped save Toyland).

Disney also released the Mickey Mouse cartoon *The Pet Shop* on October 28, 1933, roughly eight months after *King Kong* was released. Mickey gets a job at a pet shop filled with an odd assortment of animals including an ostrich. Minnie stops by to visit and after the obligatory song finds herself in danger from Beppo the Movie Monk.

Beppo, who was loaned out to appear in films, has been amusing himself in his cage by flipping through a recent movie magazine. He runs across a drawing of the actual first advertisement for the movie *King Kong* and is inspired to escape from his cage and grab Minnie.

Mickey and the other animals try to rescue Minnie, but Beppo carries her high up a stack of bird-seed boxes resembling the Empire State Building. Beppo swats away the birds circling around him like the planes in the film.

Finally, Minnie is saved and Beppo finds his head stuck in a cage with a pair of skunks. Mickey and Minnie run away before the owner returns from his lunch and finds all the destruction.

Just a few years later, RKO (which made *King Kong*) would start distributing Disney cartoons for the next two decades.

In 1931, someone at the naval reserve aviation base at Floyd Bennett Field in New York created an unlicensed design of Mickey Mouse to use on its planes. The emblem depicted Mickey riding atop a large goose with flight googles (representing a bomber) that had a bomb and a navy trident. The Statue of Liberty was in silhouette in the background.

In December 1932, RKO Studios contacted the navy wanting four navy Helldivers for one day's filming to last approximately two-and-a-half hours. The navy denied the request. Later, a representative from RKO contacted the commanding officer of Floyd Benett Field directly.

RKO would donate a hundred dollars to the Officer's Mess Fund and pay the pilots ten dollar each to fly their planes around the Empire State Building. The commanding officer accepted the offer, not knowing the request had been previously denied. Four Curtiss O2C-1 Helldivers participated.

Lieutenant John Winston recalled that he and three other pilots were given orders to "go and jazz the Empire State Building." It took the pilots less than fifteen minutes to accomplish their mission. Winston recalled:

> We didn't know what it was all about. They just said there was some kind of movie being made.

The fuselage of each plane sported the squadron's unofficial Mickey Mouse emblem and it can be clearly seen several times in *King Kong*. The pilots flew around the Empire State Building while RKO cameramen captured the footage of the planes flying in formation, peeling off and diving at an imaginary target and then looping back in the opposite direction.

RKO intercut twenty-eight scenes of the navy aircraft with process shots and miniatures featuring the logo to create the illusion of Kong being attacked by the planes.

Mickey Mouse Balloons

Just as popular as Mickey Mouse ears are the colorful helium balloons with three bubbles that resemble Mickey Mouse's head. These latex balloons came in red, blue, yellow, green, and pink with an image of Mickey's face imprinted on the largest bubble when they were first introduced in Disneyland in 1955.

Nat Lewis Balloon Company, a Disneyland park lessee at the time, handled the sales of the balloons. Rubio Arts currently handles the balloon concession.

Lewis took six of his "Disneyland Balloon Boys" to Walt Disney World for the grand opening in 1971 where 50,000 balloons were released as part of the ceremonies.

From 1961–1965, the Mickey balloons had black ears. The machinery to create these balloons no longer exists, so for the feature film *Saving Mr. Banks* (2013) over 750 balloons had to be individually hand dipped so they would be appropriate for the time period in the film. Foil balloons became popular in the early 1990s but were eliminated because of issues with overhead electrical wires.

Today, the Mickey head balloon in a clear round bubble latex balloon, known as the "glasshouse," was introduced in 1999. Creators Henry Unger and Treb Heining (one of Nate Lewis's original balloon boys) invented it specifically to be sold in Disney theme parks where they remain a favorite today.

Mickey Mouse Revue

The signature attraction at the Magic Kingdom in Florida when it opened in 1971 was a show featuring over eighty audio-animatronic Disney animated characters called the Mickey Mouse Revue created primarily by Disney artist Bill Justice, who recalled in 1999:

> [Walt Disney Imagineering] had designed some imaginative shows for the parks, but we seemed to be getting away from our heritage. What we needed was a reminder of what Walt had accomplished. I pulled out a sheet of paper and got to work. Mickey Mouse would have to be the main figure.
>
> The show we had in mind was this: Mickey Mouse would lead an orchestra of studio characters through a medley of Disney tunes. Then on the sides of the stage and behind the orchestra, scenes from our most popular animated features would appear one by one. Mickey and his orchestra would close the performance.
>
> One big problem surfaced: Mickey. With 33 functions crammed into a 42-inch body, he was the most complex audio-animatronic figure to date. He also became my biggest programming challenge because I had to do extreme movements so it would appear that Mickey was keeping up with the tempo.

An eight-minute pre-show featured an overview of Mickey's career as well as the use of sound in animation.

The attraction closed at Walt Disney World on September 14, 1980, and was moved to Tokyo Disneyland where it was an opening day attraction April 1983 and operated until May 2009.

At the Magic Kingdom, the building eventually became the home to another Mickey attraction, Mickey's PhilharMagic, that opened in 2003.

PhilharMagic is a 4-D attraction, meaning that in addition to a 3-D film, there are other elements like scents, water effects, and a 3-D moving figure in the theater.

The twelve-minute film was written by Alex Mann and directed by George Scribner, who directed the animated feature *Oliver and Company* (1988). It recounts the misadventures after Donald Duck borrows Mickey Mouse's magical hat from the "Sorcerer's Apprentice" sequence of *Fantasia*. Donald is swept away into several different Disney animated features scenarios as he tries to catch the errant hat.

Although the premise is that Mickey Mouse will be conducting the PhilharMagic Orchestra at the Fantasyland Concert Hall just as he had led several orchestras in his short cartoons, Mickey appears just briefly at the beginning and the end of the show. Wayne Allwine supplied the voice for Mickey Mouse.

Mickey Mouse Costumed Training Instructions (1973)

While Mickey Mouse as a costumed character was at Disneyland from the very beginning on July 17, 1955, training was informal for the first decade or so. By the late 1960s with improvements in costuming and increased character interaction with guests, things became more formalized.

In 1971, Alex Goldstab and Fred Duffy relocated from working with the characters in Disneyland to establishing a Disney character department in Florida for the Magic Kingdom. They started with more than two hundred character performers and realized that training needed to become more standardized.

Choreographed movements for specific characters, practice in reproducing an approved autograph signature for a particular character, and guidelines on how to handle the costumes and interactions with guests were instituted. Training books were prepared as well as videos. Here is an excerpt from the 1973 training video for the cast member assisting in the portrayal of Mickey Mouse.

> Remember while you are in costume, the reputation of Mickey Mouse and of Walt Disney Productions depends on you. You are the pixie dust which keeps the spirit of Walt Disney alive.
>
> Mickey Mouse has a glorious history. *Steamboat Willie* in 1928 portrayed Mickey as a mischievous but innocent young boy. In his early days, Mickey enjoyed stirring up trouble but managed to win the hearts of millions with his boundless energy, his sense of humor and fun loving nature.
>
> Over the past forty-five years, he has played everything from a fireman to a giant killer, from an inventor to a detective and from a cowboy to a magician. Indeed, Mickey has become an international personality and is

known and loved all over the world as the single official host of Walt Disney Productions.

Our Mickey Mouse is an average young boy of no particular age, clean-living, fun-loving, bashful around girls, polite, brave, and clever. He is not a clown nor silly or dumb.

Mickey would never lose his temper or do anything dishonest or sneaky. When he is among children, he loves to have fun with them and possesses all the energy and curiosity of a young boy.

Among dignitaries, Mickey is extremely humble and will politely shake hands. He is the symbol of the Disney company, of everything that Walt Disney created in the past and for everything he hoped for in the future. Mickey Mouse represents a unique era in motion pictures, art, television, animation and design.

Most importantly, this little character represents a spirit of happiness, laughter, harmony, and friendship to millions of people all over the world. Undoubtedly, Mickey Mouse is the most famous of all Disney characters.

As you go out to greet your audience, remember the voice of Mickey Mouse is easily recognized and children are not fooled by imitations. So, while you are in costume, the first rule is that you not talk. Most important to remember is to the children, Mickey Mouse is real. The fact that there is a person in the costume should never be revealed.

You have an amazing power, for with a mere handshake and gentle hug, you can bring a smile to a care-worn face, a sparkle to a child's eye, or some long-needed joy into a tired life. You are responsible for the unique happiness which families discover when they visit your Disney home.

Brief History of Costumed Theme Park Character

At the opening of Disneyland on July 17, 1955, host Art Linkletter told television audiences:

> Dumbo, Pluto, and Donald Duck and all the other characters are from the Walt Disney costumes created for John Harris' *Ice Capades* which is on tour right now around the United States.

In 1949, *Ice Capades*, a touring ice skating show produced by John H. Harris, partnered with the Disney studio to showcase a lengthy segment in each year's show that would feature Disney characters. This partnership lasted through 1966.

Walt Disney attended the Ice Capades productions, watching the Disney-inspired segments closely. He noticed that audiences just accepted the costumes as the characters with a willing suspension of disbelief.

However, the costumes were designed to provide flexibility for the skater so they followed the contours of the person's body and human, not cartoon, proportions.

In addition, they had to be designed to allow the greatest visibility which explains the horrid teeth on Mickey Mouse on Disneyland's opening day, since the mesh between the spiky chompers was necessary for peripheral vision.

These costumes were meant, like most theatrical costumes, to be viewed briefly at a distance under proper lighting, not inspected up close and at length by Disneyland guests.

It was impractical for Disneyland to keep borrowing those costumes, so the Disney studio costume shop tried to make their own based on the Ice Capades examples but trying to improve the appearance. These newer versions turned out to be extraordinarily heavy, awkward, and at times, unprofessional with flashes of real skin like a wrist or neck being common.

Imagineer John Hench recalled:

> Mickey's transformation from 2-D to 3-D worlds was natural, except for the design, of course. It is actually astonishing that Mickey held his identity. Making him a real, live character represented a violent shift that violated the head-to-body proportions [of the 2-D character].
>
> After a time, we made our own costumes for the walk-around characters. Of course, we got better at it as we went along. For example, we found smaller people [to wear the costumes] who didn't distort the image so much. The first characters weren't that great, I guess.

Ron Logan, former executive vice-president of Walt Disney Entertainment, said:

> Because height ranges for the characters had not been established, Mickey was sometimes over six feet tall! In the fall of 1961 that all changed through the contributions of Bill Justice and John Hench who brought a higher quality design and consistency to the characters.
>
> At Walt's personal request, a new Mickey Mouse costume was designed by John Hench. Walt wanted to cast a smaller performer as Mickey and standardize the performer's height in costume. Paul Castle [who had performed in the *Ice Capades* as Mickey and other Disney characters like Dopey for years] was personally selected by Walt to perform the role.

Disney animator Bill Justice said:

> When Disneyland opened, we needed characters to meet the public regularly. Everything had to be redesigned to more accurately represent the characters and stand up to the rigors of everyday use among the guests.
>
> Walt told me, "Other places can have thrill rides and bands and trains. Only we have our characters." The costumed characters were very important to Walt. He said, "Bill, always remember we don't want to torture the people

who are wearing them. Keep in mind they've got to be as comfortable as possible. Try to get the lightest weight materials and the most ventilation as possible." The first concern was always safety and the second was accuracy.

Logan stated:
> In the early years, the characters walked around Disneyland freely, greeting guests and posing for pictures. There was no schedule shared with the guests so there was no guarantee that the guests might see them. It was all serendipity.

Animator Ward Kimball said:
> People's perception of Mickey Mouse is the one they see at [Disneyland]. That's the one they meet with their children. He's got long pants. He's got extra eyebrows... more like the stuffed dolls they sell [than how he ever appeared in any cartoon].

Continual improvements were made on the costumes to make them lighter, more flexible, and accurate. More formal training procedures were introduced including how to write a consistent autograph.

In 2010, an interactive Mickey Mouse head was introduced to the Disney theme parks where Mickey blinked his eyes, moved his mouth, and by 2013 was able to talk with guests. The Talking Mickey costume, because it must support a head with the mechanics to move the mouth, nose, and eyes to support the illusion of speech, is heavier and wears out more quickly than a regular Mickey costume.

However, the increased costs for tech and labor compared to a "regular" Mickey became too expensive and the talking version was removed in 2018.

Men Behind the Mouse: Paul Castle

When Mickey Mouse pounded on the huge drum in Fantasy on Parade down Disneyland's Main Street for thousands of times, it was Paul Castle. When Mickey Mouse received his star on the Hollywood Boulevard Walk of Fame, it was Paul Castle.

When Mickey Mouse cavorted at the 1964 New York World's Fair, it was Paul Castle. When Walt appeared in his final photo in front of Sleeping Beauty Castle with Mickey Mouse waving, it was Paul Castle.

From 1961 to 1986, when he officially retired, Castle would refer to himself as the "Main Mickey" and it would be hard to argue with that designation.

At just four feet six inches tall, he had a long career as a novelty ice skater with both Holiday on Ice and the Ice Capades shows. He amazed audiences as the world's smallest barrel jumper—able to jump over fifteen feet of obstacles like barrels or suitcases.

Castle said:

> Walt Disney saw how good I did as Disney characters. I'd first met him when I did *Snow White and the Seven Dwarfs* [in the 1958 Ice Capades, Castle is credited in the program as performing as Dopey].

Walt wanted a small but highly animated Mickey for Disneyland and hired Castle.

Abby Disney, the granddaughter of Roy O. Disney, recalled meeting Castle backstage at Disneyland when she was a child:

> Just outside the employee's parking lot, there was a little cafeteria outside for the employees. I looked over and saw Mickey having a cup of coffee with Snow White. His head was on the table and he was smoking a big cigar. He was very short and old and had this gravelly deep voice.

He came over to my grandmother and gave her a big hug. "Edna! Edna! Glad to see ya!" That's how I remember Mickey Mouse; he's emblazoned on my brain that way.

Castle told a reporter for the *Los Angeles Times* in January 1988:

> My most favorite time of all was with Walt Disney in the Rose Parade in 1966, the year he passed away. He was the grand marshal of the Rose Parade and I was in the car with him in the back seat, just Walt and I for three hours. Just Walt and I. Of all the things I've done in my lifetime, that to me was my biggest day. Walt and me, January 1, 1966.

Paul Castle died in 2010 at the age of 86.

'Earforce One'

Earforce One was created for Walt Disney World's 15th anniversary in 1986. It was a ten-story-high hot-air balloon in the shape of Mickey Mouse's head that was inspired by the much smaller helium Mickey Mouse balloons sold in the Disney parks.

Earforce One measured 96 feet from the bottom of its basket to the top of Mickey's head. Each ear was 35 feet in diameter; the nose snout was 33 feet long, each eye 16.5 feet high, and the 54.6 foot diameter head measured 168.3 feet in circumference. Uninflated and minus the basket, the balloon weighed roughly 330 pounds.

The huge mouse-eared balloon was manufactured by Cameron Balloons Ltd. of Bristol, England, noted for producing many odd-shaped balloons since 1971.

A typical hot air balloon is made up of about 200 pieces of special purpose nylon fabric drawn from 6 to 20 patterns. Earforce One was much more complicated, with 500 pieces drawn from 50 patterns. The pilots for that first tour were Robert Carlton and David Justice. Earforce One also toured the nation (including visiting Disneyland) in 1988 to celebrate Mickey's 60th birthday that year.

To celebrate the 50th anniversary of Disneyland, a newer version of the original Earforce One (that had been decommissioned many years earlier) was created by Cameron Balloons and dubbed the Happiest Balloon on Earth in 2006. It was unique because Mickey sported a "golden ears" souvenir cap like the one guests could purchase at Disneyland.

The balloon was approximately 113,000 cubic feet in volume. It stood 98 feet tall and spanned 53 feet from ear-to-ear. Since Mickey's nose is 5.5 feet in diameter, an average child could easily stand up inside it. 2,000 averaged-sized children could fit inside the inflated balloon. If Mickey's proportionate body were added to the balloon, he would stand more than 200 feet tall.

It was the first hot air balloon to ever rise over the Grand Canyon and even flew below the rim of the Grand Canyon on April 11, 2006, a much trickier maneuver due to air currents.

The balloon was built for a 14-stop tour, including cities like San Francisco to showcase it against the backdrop of the Golden Gate Bridge. After the last stop on the tour, July 17, 2006, at Disneyland, the balloon was returned to Cameron Balloons to replace the gold ears with black ones. Many invitation requests for its use come in from local festivals and balloon rallies.

Mickey Imposter: Mickey at 60

Illustrator William Stout told interviewer Steve Ringgenberg in 1996:

> The first book of *Mickey at 60* was done while I was working at Walt Disney Imagineering. I kept hearing all this Mickey's 60th birthday hype and I thought, "He hasn't done a picture in years. He's probably let himself go. He's living in a little bungalow in Hollywood. Minnie's probably divorced him and is living off her alimony in Miami."
>
> I drew this little sort of overweight, grungy version of what Mickey might look like now. And it got a great reaction at work, and so I started to draw these strips to hand around. I would draw a whole page full of *Mickey at 60* comic strips and then pass it to my friend Jim Steinmeyer [another Imagineer] and I would leave the word balloons blank and he would fill in the word balloons. You know, it really is not so much a satire of Mickey Mouse, as it's really a satire of almost every Hollywood movie star I've ever met who's sort of living in his past.

When Stout realized he and Steinmeyer had quite a collection of these "anti-comics," he Xeroxed off 300 signed copies with cardstock covers and sold them for fifteen dollars each at the San Diego Comic Con. They sold out in the first two hours. They donated all of the money to the Crippled Children's Society.

That first issue was barely twenty-four pages of artwork and begins with a three-page comic-book sequence to set up the concept and then each page after that has five strips covering everything from Mickey's agent to his vacation in Las Vegas to his appearance on Johnny Carson. Even CEO Michael Eisner requested a copy and sent a nice complimentary note in return.

After Stout left Disney, he and Steinmeyer kept in touch and in 1996, they produced a second volume of *Mickey at 60*. It is almost twice the size of the first volume with Mickey Mouse running for president, doing his taxes, the tax audit, visiting Paris, his trip to the unemployment office, his book tour, and his jury duty. The proceeds from this second volume benefited the Clear View School, a school for mentally disturbed children. This edition was limited to 950 copies and 50 artist's proof copies. Stout has roughed out ideas for a third volume and notes for a live one-man theater show with the character.

Stout recently remembered:

> You know, it really is not so much a satire of Mickey Mouse, as it's really a satire of almost every Hollywood movie star I've ever met who's sort of living in his past.
>
> I'd love to do a volume three. I've roughed out some ideas already. It takes time, though—both mine and Jim's. (Among other things Steinmeyer went on to design the effects for the Mary Poppins stage production.)
>
> I also began writing a "Mickey at 60" one-man show for our mutual friend Roger Cox (an Imagineer who worked on creating the Adventurer's Club for Pleasure Island). Roger's death took a lot of the wind out of the sails of that project. I would still like to get back to it and finish it. I think it would make a great one-man show and a hilarious "autobiographical" (from Mickey's point of view) graphic novel.
>
> There was even talk of including "Mickey at 60" as a presence in the Comedy Warehouse (a club I helped to design) for Pleasure Island. I drew up "Mickey at 60" drink napkins and Jim wrote hilarious word balloon dialogue for them. They were never manufactured, however. It seemed strange and ironic that WDI was going to license our "Mickey at 60" character from us.

LiMOUSEine

In the spring of 1989, to promote the opening of Disney-MGM Studios, the "LimMOUSEine" with a costumed Mickey Mouse and Walt Disney World Ambassador Kathleen Sullivan departed Orlando on March 5, 1989, for an almost-40 city East Coast tour, beginning in Indianapolis, that would last for roughly four months.

The driver of the unique burgundy stretch limo was Bill Marable, a former Disney bus driver, who often had to maneuver through narrow and awkward turns during the trip. The six-wheeled vehicle was loaded with high technology, since it was supposed to represent Mickey's "home away from home."

Its actual weight was about 7,980 pounds, but the electronics added approximately 1,000 pounds. The length was 40 feet, and overall width 79.5 inches. The height was 65 inches with a wheelbase of 331 inches.

This five-door vehicle sat a dozen passengers comfortably, but was placed low to the ground to accommodate the size of the costumed Disney characters. There were yards of windows and four oversized glass sunroofs with sliding shades, large enough for the characters to stand up and wave to guests.

Billed as "the longest fixed-frame vehicle that can be driven legally on U.S. roads," the super-limo included electronic gear (much of it donated by Sony and considered top-of-the-line at the time). The base vehicle for the LiMOUSEine was a Lincoln Town Car cut in half and stretched more than 20 feet on a beefed-up frame.

The interior included an entertainment center with AM-FM stereo cassette player, CD player, 20 speakers, 8mm videocassette player, a half-inch Beta videocassette player, and two eight-inch Trinitron color monitors with wireless remote. Passengers could watch television programs received by antenna or watch videos. Two cellular telephones with separate lines could be used from four different locations in the car.

The Rolls-Royce front end with gold-plated radiator shell and trim had a 24-karat Mickey three-circled head shape. There were custom-built Mickey ears over front wheel wells, sparkling shooting-star effects on both front doors, 12 external parade speakers for parades and drive-up fanfares (with 1,200 watts of amplifier), and red carpet and hook-ups for external power when parked with the engine off.

Designed by Disney artist Tom Tripodi, at a cost of more than $100,000, the LiMOUSEine was built by Ultra Corp. of Brea, California, from a potpourri of car parts. Ultra was renowned for building limos for celebrities.

Mickey on 'The Mickey Mouse Club' (1955–1958)

Disney animators Bill Justice and X. Atencio formed a separate animation unit at the Disney studio to do the opening of the original *Mickey Mouse Club* television show at the personal request of Walt Disney who insisted the new animation be filmed in color even though it would be aired in black and white.

The show opening was two minutes, forty seconds with animation to the now familiar theme song written by MMC performer Jimmie Dodd, the "Mickey Mouse March," that began: "Who's the leader of the club that's made for you and me?"

Mickey's individual introduction, in a different outfit for each day of the week, was roughly twenty-five seconds. The closing animation of Mickey saying good-bye was ten seconds. Walt came out of his self-imposed retirement to supply the voice for Mickey. It would be the last time he did Mickey's voice professionally.

MONDAY: *Fun With Music Day.* Mickey dressed in straw hat and striped jacket like a Main Street, U.S.A. Dapper Dan animated by Ollie Johnston

TUESDAY: *Guest Star Day.* Mickey dressed in tuxedo with white tie animated by Ollie Johnston

WEDNESDAY: *Anything Can Happen Day.* Mickey dressed in his "Sorcerer's Apprentice" outfit animated by Hal King. (Mickey's robe is purple in the color version of this opening rather than red.)

THURSDAY: *Circus Day.* Mickey dressed in a red bandleader outfit animated by Hal King.

FRIDAY: *Talent Round-Up.* Mickey dressed as a rope twirling cowboy animated by John Lounsberry.

Near the last quarter of the show, different Mouseketeers would stand in front of the Mickey Mouse Treasure Mine and chant the following song, again written by Dodd, to open the doors to find the name of the day's Mousekartoon.

> Time to twist the mouse-ka-dial to the right and the left with a great big smile.
> This is the way we get to see a Mouse-kar-toon for you and me.
> Mee-ska! Moose-ka! Mouse-ke-teer! Mouse-kar-toon time now is here!

The Mousekartoon segment was very popular during the first season since it was one of the few opportunities to see Mickey Mouse short cartoons in the decades before videotape, running every day during the last quarter of the show and featuring cartoons from 1929–1936.

During the second season, the cartoons were reduced to four days a week with two dozen repeats from the first season. More Donald Duck cartoons were shown, and the selection was from 1938–1948. For the third season, the cartoons were cut down to once (and sometimes twice) a week, with more Pluto cartoons and the selection from 1939–1952. All were edited and broadcast in black and white.

There was a special five-episode segment entitled "Karen in Kartoonland" where popular Mouseketeer Karen Pendleton would visit a Disney artist to learn how to draw. The February 2, 1956, segment had her visiting Bill Justice who showed her how to draw Mickey Mouse and had her model facial expressions that he then duplicated on Mickey's face.

Mickey Cartoons: First Mickey Mouse Animated TV Commercials

Phyllis Hurrell, Walt Disney's niece, set up a small area at the Disney studio and was the television commercial coordinator from 1954-1957. Using Disney animators and facilities, she produced commercials for a number of clients including 7-Up, Ipana Toothpaste, and Mohawk Carpets.

Commercials for American Motors (a sponsor of the Disneyland weekly television show with a pavilion at the Disneyland theme park, Circarama) featured Disney characters hawking Nash Ramblers and the Ambassador.

Artist Tom Oreb redesigned the classic Disney characters with a more streamlined look for the series of American Motors commercials. Mickey was given a big "adult" suit and a triangular face in the UPA animation style of the time.

One commercial had Pluto napping by his doghouse when he is hit by an advertising flier for the 1955 Nash Ambassador and Statesman that he takes to Mickey Mouse who is relaxing in a hammock.

Pluto is distracted by a cat eating out of his bowl and chases the feline through the yard and into the garage while the announcer (Bill Ewing) extols the benefits of how the car can turn and has a nice big windshield (since Pluto now has his head stuck in a fishbowl). Mickey is convinced and ready to walk out and go to the car lot and takes Pluto along.

Clarence "Ducky" Nash supplied the voice for Mickey Mouse in this ninety-second commercial directed by Nick Nichols that was completed November 29, 1954.

Victor Haboush, who did background design on

a number of these commercials, told animation historian Amid Amidi that when the Nash commercial aired with Mickey Mouse:

> There was a kid that used to write Walt telling him to stay away from modern art because it's communistic. So when the commercial came on, he wrote in to complain and Walt went crazy.
>
> He stormed down there and outlawed us against using any of the Disney characters in commercials. It basically spelled the end of the unit. [Companies] were coming for the celebrity, to be able to use Disney characters in commercials.

These commercials were animated by regular Disney animators Jerry Hathcock (who did much of the work on all the Disney commercials), George Nicholas, and George Kreisl. The Mickey commercials featured layout and character design by Tom Oreb. There are at least three other American Motors commercials with Mickey that aired in 1955.

Mickey Loves a Parade

Mickey Mouse was the grand marshal for the 116th Tournament of Roses Parade in Pasadena, California, on New Year's Day 2005. He was the first cartoon character to receive the honor.

In announcing that Mickey would be the grand marshal, Tournament of Roses president Dave Davis said:

> Mickey Mouse has brought entertainment, joy and laughter to families around the world for 75 years and we couldn't think of a more ideal Grand Marshall to help us "Celebrate Family" in 2005. He is a friend to families around the world.

A costumed Mickey Mouse accompanied Grand Marshal Walt Disney in the 1966 Rose Parade.

The first Macy's Thanksgiving Parade Mickey Mouse balloon appeared in 1934 and was a collaborative effort between Walt Disney and Macy's Tony Sarg. It was forty feet tall (containing 2,664 cubic feet of helium) and lasted through 1939.

Mickey in an open-collared yellow shirt appeared in 1972 to celebrate the first anniversary of Walt Disney World. Mickey returned again in 1973 to mark 50 years of Disney cartoons. In 2000, a new Bandleader Mickey balloon was introduced. Sailor Mickey debuted in the parade in 2009 and 2010 to mark the announcement of the *Disney Dream* and *Disney Fantasy* cruise ships.

Mickey Moments

- In 1949, on the verge of the Korean War, the U.S. Army asked a group of prominent Koreans to suggest what sign over the door of its information center would immediately tell their countrymen it was American. "After a brief consultation, the Koreans' vote went 100 percent for Mickey Mouse" stated *Collier's* magazine, April 9, 1949.

- Excerpts from Mickey Mouse cartoons appeared in movies from other studios. A short clip from *Ye Olden Days* (1933) is seen at the beginning of the Fox Films *My Lips Betray* (1933). Republic Pictures Corporation film *Michael O'Halloran* (1937) features an excerpt from *Puppy Love* (1933). In Paramount's *Sullivan's Travels* (1941) is an excerpt from *Playful Pluto* (1934).

- A music colleague approached conductor Leopold Stokowski, who appeared in *Fantasia* (1940), and said, "I'll bet you don't know why I admire you so much. It's because you're the only man I know who shook hands with Mickey Mouse!" Stokowski wagged his finger at his friend and replied, "No! No! No! *He* shook hands with *me*."

- In 1937, on his ninth birthday, the Boy Scouts of America bestowed upon Mickey membership in the Cub Scouts.

- At the end of December 1980, Disneyland in Anaheim, California, received an official government letter addressed to Mickey Mouse. Inside was a form letter requesting that Mickey send in his correct birth date information so he could be properly registered for the draft.

Mickey Cartoons: 'Sorcerer Mickey'

As the "Sorcerer's Apprentice" segment began to develop for *Fantasia* (1940), Dopey from *Snow White and the Seven Dwarfs* (1937) was suggested for the apprentice role, but Walt felt it would a great showcase for Mickey Mouse. Some of the elements from Dopey's costume in *Snow White* remain in *Fantasia* including the over-sized sleeves that would slip over his hands, the long robe with the distinctive neckline, and the soft brown shoes.

The original story continuity at the time stated that it was "a picture of a typical little man and what he would like to do once given complete control of the earth and its elements. In his dream Mickey is having a spectacular lot of fun without being malicious."

Walt saw Mickey as an orchestra conductor who in a dream was directing the ocean and the stars. For layout, he suggested:

> Have a lot of up-shots, looking up at the guy, you know, like you'd shoot up at an orchestra conductor as he is conducting.

Director Jim Algar began handing out the first scenes to animate on January 21, 1938, with Preston Blair being given the scene of Mickey waking from the dream in an armchair surrounded by water. Edward Love and George Rowley worked on the never-ending brooms.

Les Clark did much of the animation of Mickey along with Riley Thompson—in particular, he did the sections from the first appearance of Mickey with buckets in hand until the end of the dream. Cy Young animated Mickey carried off by the waves.

Fred Moore helped with the design of Mickey to make him "conform to a cute style" and the animators were directed to consult with him.

Fantasia premiered on November 13, 1940, at the Broadway Theater in New York, the same theater that premiered *Steamboat Willie* almost exactly twelve years earlier on November 18. Several New York film critics singled out Mickey's segment as the best part of the film. Disney animator Woolie Reitherman stated:

> [Mickey in] "The Sorcerer's Apprentice" was a very charming thing but to me it started the trend of Mickey where he became a different kind of character from that little flip guy that was always fighting off Peg-Leg Pete and all these impossible things, with Minnie and all that stuff. There was a charm, a naïve quality [to those shorts].

A Dozen Appearances of Sorcerer Mickey

TELEVISION:

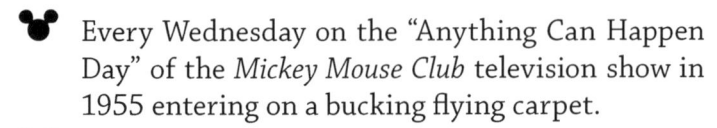

- Every Wednesday on the "Anything Can Happen Day" of the *Mickey Mouse Club* television show in 1955 entering on a bucking flying carpet.

- *The House of Mouse* television series including the episode "Mickey and Minnie's Big Vacation" where he has to save the nightclub from a flood caused by Donald Duck. In *Mickey's House of Villains*, Mickey has to transform into Sorcerer Mickey to save the nightclub after it has been taken over by villains like Captain Hook, Jafar and Cruella De Vil.

VIDEO GAMES:

- Sorcerer Mickey appears in video games like *Kingdom Hearts 3D: Dream Drop Distance* and *Epic Mickey 2: The Power of Two* as well as *Disney Infinity*.

LOGO:

- Sorcerer Mickey was the mascot icon for Walt Disney Home Video and its home video releases beginning in 1987.

- Sorcerer Mickey was also the icon for Walt Disney Imagineering beginning in the late 1990s and continuing until today.

- Sorcerer Mickey is the mascot for the *Disney Dream* cruise ship launched in 2011 with a full three-dimensional figure of him decorating the stern of the ship along with his mischievous brooms.

- Sorcerer Mickey was the logo for the 25th anniversary celebration of Walt Disney World in 1996.

PARKS:

- A forty-five-foot-tall inflatable Sorcerer Mickey balloon was one of the parade floats for Disneyland's Party Gras Parade from January 1990 to November 1990 as part of the 35th birthday celebration for the park.
- Sorcerer Mickey was the unofficial mascot of Disney's Hollywood Studios (formerly Disney-MGM Studios) since *Fantasia* came out in 1940 and the park was meant to represent the Hollywood of the 1930s and 1940s. A statue of Sorcerer Mickey is in the Mickey's of Hollywood store on Hollywood Boulevard.
- Sorcerer Mickey appears in the finale of the nighttime entertainment spectacular *Fantasmic!*
- Unveiled at the end of Hollywood Boulevard at Disney's Hollywood Studios on October 1, 2001, as part of the "100 Years of Magic Celebration," was a 100-foot-tall iconic sorcerer hat that Mickey wore in the film *Fantasia* and which weighed 27 tons.
- As part of the Millennium Celebration in 2000, a twenty-five-story Sorcerer Mickey's arm and hand that held a gigantic magic wand with "starfetti" was installed next to Spaceship Earth in Epcot.

Men Behind the Mouse: Paul Murry

Paul Murry joined the Disney studio in 1938 and was an assistant to animator Fred Moore. He worked on several Disney animated features including some work on the "Sorcerer's Apprentice" segment of *Fantasia* (1940).

He quit the Disney studio in 1946 and began doing freelance work for the Disney-related Dell comic books produced by Western Publishing, drawing every character from Snow White to Humphrey the Bear. Murry is best known for doing the artwork on twenty years of the Mickey Mouse serial adventures in the back of *Walt Disney's Comics and Stories* beginning with "The Last Resort" in WDCS #152 (May 1953) and ending in July 1973 with "Flight of the Dragon" in WDCS #394. After the serials ended, he continued to draw eight-page stories with Mickey until his retirement around 1984. He died in 1989.

His first Mickey Mouse story, "Mickey Mouse and the Monster Whale," was a 24-page feature in *Vacation Parade* #1 (1950). Perhaps his oddest Mickey Mouse assignment was *Mickey Mouse* issues #107 through #109 in 1966. Murry drew the cartoony Mickey and Goofy in stories that had realistic backgrounds and realistic human beings drawn by Dan Spiegle (who drew many of the television and movie Disney adaptations for Dell). Mickey and Goofy were secret agents for Police International, an attempt to try to take advantage of the then-popular spy craze.

Murry was also responsible for redrawing pages or panels of Floyd Gottfredson's newspaper strips, when they were reprinted, to update Mickey's appearance, soften unacceptable violence, or trim the length of the story.

In a 1982 interview with Klaus Spillman, Murry said:
> I did primarily pencil art only for my comic-book stories. I never wrote any of the scripts. Because I had formerly been an assistant to Fred Moore, the animator who made Mickey Mouse what he is today, I was particularly drawn to doing Mickey rather than characters like the Ducks.
>
> I used to work roughly six months in advance of publication and got paid about twelve dollars a page. I didn't pay much attention to what other [comic-book] artists were doing. I've cut back because at my age I prefer not to spend all my time drawing Mickey Mouse. I just don't think the stories are as good today. I don't know why they stopped the serials. I enjoyed doing them.

The Chaplin Mouse

In *The American Magazine* for March 1931, Walt Disney described Mickey's creation:

> I think we were rather indebted to Charlie Chaplin for the idea. We wanted something appealing and we thought of a tiny bit of a mouse that would have something of the wistfulness of Chaplin—a little fellow trying to do the best he could.

The Little Tramp and the early Mickey Mouse did have several superficial similarities. They played multiple different parts in different locations yet always remained the same easily recognized character at their core. They were the "little fellow" who was the poor underdog during the Great Depression who stood up against physically larger authority figures and usually got the girl.

Alva Johnston, after an interview with Walt Disney, stated:

> Chaplin was a kind of godfather to Mickey Mouse. It is now and always has been the aim of Disney to graft the psychology of Chaplin upon Mickey. The two universal characters have something in common in their approach to their problems. They have the same blend of hero and coward, nitwit and genius, mug and gentleman.

The Firefighters (1930) includes elements like the fire engine falling apart piece by piece on the way to the emergency, as it did in Chaplin's *The Fireman* (1916). The end of *The Klondike Kid* (1932) was inspired by a similar gag with a teetering shack in the frozen north from Chaplin's *The Gold Rush* (1925) but with a particular Disney twist at the end.

Other sight gags from Chaplin films were incorporated into early Mickey cartoons as well, including cranking a cow's tail later used by Mickey cranking a goat's tail in a similar fashion in *Steamboat Willie* (1928). To entertain an orphan mouse left on his doorstep, Mickey briefly imitates Chaplin in a scene animated by Bob Wickersham in *Mickey Plays Papa* (1934) and amusingly, the tyke is unimpressed.

Mickey's Gala Premiere (1933) features caricatures of roughly forty movie stars including Chaplin's Little Tramp attending the premiere of a new Mickey Mouse cartoon.

In *Mickey's Polo Team* (1936), the Mickey Mousers team consists of Mickey, Donald Duck, Goofy, and the Big Bad Wolf. The Hollywood team of movie stars includes Charlie Chaplin, Oliver Hardy, Stan Laurel, and Harpo Marx. Chaplin enters on a polo pony with the same black curly hair, derby, mustache, shoes, and attitude as Charlie.

As Chaplin became more controversial and less popular, his influence and appearances in Disney cartoons faded.

The University of the Air (NBC Radio Broadcast Fall 1948)

From 1944–1948, *The University of the Air* radio series produced in Chicago by NBC had thirty-minute episodes that presented adaptations of the world's greatest novels. In 1948, the production was moved to Hollywood and expanded to sixty minutes and lasted until early 1951.

While the adaptations continued, the episodes now sometimes included short interviews as well. Walt's interview was late in 1948 to publicize Mickey's twentieth birthday which was celebrated anytime during the fall season to publicize Disney's latest theatrical release or encourage theaters to hold birthday parties and rent multiple cartoon shorts

WALT DISNEY: "Mickey Mouse to me is the symbol of independence. Born of necessity, the little fellow provided the means for expanding our organization to its present dimensions and for extending the medium of cartoon animation toward new entertainment levels.

"He has appeared in more pictures than any flesh-and-blood star. He was the first cartoon character to express personality and to be constantly kept in character. I thought of him from the first as a distinct individual not just a cartoon type or symbol going through a comedy routine.

"Of course, sound had a very considerable effect on our treatment of Mickey Mouse. It gave his character a new dimension. It rounded him into complete life-likeness. In the early days, I did the voice of Mickey [because] it wasn't financially feasible to hire people for such assignments.

"Mickey had reached the state where we had to be very careful about what we permitted him to do. He'd become a hero in the eyes of his audiences, especially the youngsters. Mickey could do no wrong. I could never attribute any meanness or callous traits to him.

"I often find myself surprised at what has been said about our redoubtable little Mickey who was never really a mouse nor yet wholly a man, although always recognizably human, I hope.

"But all we ever intended for him and expected of him was that he should continue to make people everywhere chuckle with him and at him. We didn't burden him with any social symbolism. We made him no mouthpiece for frustrations or harsh satire. Mickey was simply a little personality assigned to the purposes of laughter.

"There is much nostalgia for me in these reflections. The life and ventures of Mickey Mouse have been closely bound up with my own personal and professional life. It is understandable that I should have sentimental attachment for the little personage who played so big a part in the course of Disney Productions and has been so happily accepted as an amusing friend wherever films are show around the world. He still speaks for me and I still speak for him. Mickey, I think on this occasion you should say something to all our friends who are listening around the world."

MICKEY: "OK. Well...uh...happy birthday, everybody."

WALT: "No, no, Mickey. You don't understand. It's your birthday."

MICKEY: "Oh...gosh...well, I'll be seein' ya."

Acknowledgments

As always, I would like to acknowledge not only the people who directly helped me with this specific book, but those who have inspired or supported me over the years.

There are indeed angels in this world and I have been blessed to know so many of them and benefit from their kindness and generosity.

Special thanks to those who continue to purchase my books.

This book would not have been possible without the skills and encouragement of publisher Bob McLain and his Theme Park Press who have allowed me an amazing opportunity to share Disney history with so many others.

Thanks to my brothers, Michael and Chris, and their families including their children Amber, Keith, Autumn, and Story, and my grand-nieces Skylar, Shea, and Sidnee as well as grand nephews Alex and Max. Hopefully, one day they may think I am cool for listing their names here.

I am also indebted to all those other writers who over the decades have researched and shared their information about Mickey Mouse: David Bain, Bruce Harris, Michael Barrier, John Culhane, Pete Martin, R.H. Farber, Robert Feild, Christopher Finch, David Gerstein, Didier Ghez, John Grant, Howard E. Green, Bruce Hamilton, Robert Heide, John Gilman, John Hench, Ward Kimball, Richard Holliss, Brian Sibley, Leslie Iwerks, John Kenworthy, Kathy Merlock Jackson, Bill Justice, Keith Keller, Pierre Lambert, David Lesjak, George Grant;

Leonard Maltin, Cecil Munsey, Walton Rawls, Lorraine Santoli, Richard Shale, Bernard Shine, David R. Smith, Charles Solomon, Bob Thomas, Frank Thomas, Ollie

Johnston, Robert Tieman, David Tietyen, Garry Apgar, M. Thomas Inge, John Canemaker, Jeff Kurtti, Geoffrey Blum, Thomas Andrae, Bill Blackbeard, Peter Adamakos, Malcolm Willits, Russell Schroeder, Jim Fanning, Timothy Susanin, Steven M. Barrett, Floyd Norman, Don "Ducky" Williams.

Additional thanks in particular to Diane Disney Miller, JB Kaufman, Werner Weiss, Sam Gennawey, Kim Eggink, John Cawley, Bill Iadonisi, Tom and Marina Stern, Jerry and Liz Edwards, Lonnie Hicks, Kirk Bowman, Ryan N. March, Kaye Bundey, Greg Ehrbar;

Todd James Pierce, Betty Bjerrum, Jerry Beck, Dr. Mark Round, Dave Mruz, Tracy M. Barnes, Sarah Pate, Tamysen Hall, Evlyn Gould, Bruce Gordon, David Mumford, Randy Bright, Jack and Leon Janzen, Lou Mongello, Howard Kalov, Todd Regan, Dave Mason.

And sadly some people that I have foolishly forgotten for the moment. I hope all of you, both acknowledged and temporarily missing, live happily ever after and enjoy this book.

Finally, thanks to Walt Disney for Mickey Mouse and so much more.

About the Author

Jim Korkis is an internationally respected Disney historian who has written hundreds of articles and more than twenty books about all things Disney over the last forty years. Jim grew up in Glendale, California, where he was able to meet and interview Walt's original team of animators and Imagineers.

He was first officially identified as a Mickey Mouse authority on the April 20, 1989, episode of the television show *Entertainment Tonight*. That led to him sharing subsequent insights about the Mouse in books, magazine articles, presentations, and television shows. He authored *The Book of Mouse: A Celebration of Walt Disney's Mickey Mouse* (Theme Park Press 2013) that received praise as a valuable resource from other historians who have written books about the Mouse.

In 1995, Jim relocated to Orlando, Florida, where he worked for Walt Disney World in a variety of capacities including Entertainment, Animation, Disney Institute, Disney University, College and International Programs, Disney Cruise Line, Yellow Shoes Marketing, Disney Design Group, and Disney Vacation Club.

His original research on Disney history has been used often by the Disney company as well as other organizations including the Disney Family Museum. In September 2017, he was awarded the National Disneyana Fan Club's Heritage Award for his work in Disney scholarship.

Several websites currently frequently feature Jim's articles about Disney history:
- MousePlanet.com
- AllEars.net

- Yesterland.com
- CartoonResearch.com
- YourFirstVisit.net

In addition, Jim is a frequent guest on multiple podcasts as well as a consultant and keynote speaker to various businesses, schools, and groups.

Jim is not currently an employee of the Disney company.

To read more stories by Jim Korkis about Disney history, please check out his other books, all available from Theme Park Press:

- *More Secret Stories of Disneyland* (2018)
- *Extra Secret Stories of Walt Disney World* (2018)
- *Call Me Walt* (2017)
- *Walt's Words* (2017)
- *Secret Stories of Disneyland* (2017)
- *The Vault of Walt: Volume 6* (2018)
- *Gremlin Trouble* (2017)
- *Donald Duck's Daddy* (2017)
- *More Secret Stories of Walt Disney World* (2016)
- *The Vault of Walt: Volume 5* (2016)
- *The Unofficial Disneyland 1955 Companion* (2016)
- *How to Be a Disney Historian* (2016)
- *Secret Stories of Walt Disney World* (2015)
- *The Vault of Walt: Volume 4* (2015)
- *Everything I Know I Learned from Disney Animated Features* (2015)
- *The Vault of Walt: Volume 3* (2014)
- *Animation Anecdotes* (2014)
- *Who's the Leader of the Club? Walt Disney's Leadership Lessons* (2014)
- *The Book of Mouse* (2013)
- *The Vault of Walt: Volume 2* (2013)
- *Who's Afraid of the Song of the South?* (2012)
- *The Revised Vault of Walt* (2012)

ABOUT THEME PARK PRESS

Theme Park Press publishes books primarily about the Disney company, its history, culture, films, animation, and theme parks, as well as theme parks in general.

Our authors include noted historians, animators, Imagineers, and experts in the theme park industry.

We also publish many books by first-time authors, with topics ranging from fiction to theme park guides.

And we're always looking for new talent. If you'd like to write for us, or if you're interested in the many other titles in our catalog, please visit:

www.ThemeParkPress.com

Theme Park Press Newsletter

Subscribe to our free email newsletter and enjoy:

- Free book downloads and giveaways
- Access to excerpts from our many books
- Announcements of forthcoming releases
- Exclusive additional content and chapters
- And more good stuff available nowhere else

To subscribe, visit www.ThemeParkPress.com, or send email to newsletter@themeparkpress.com.

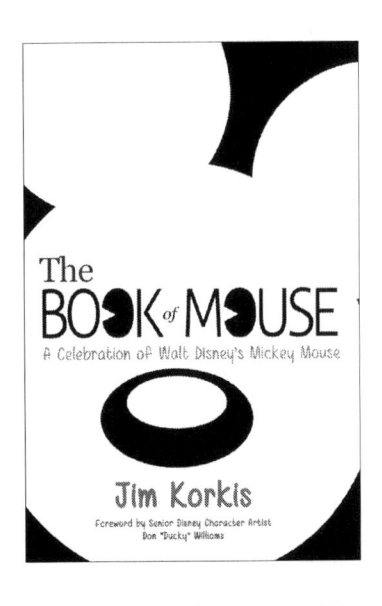

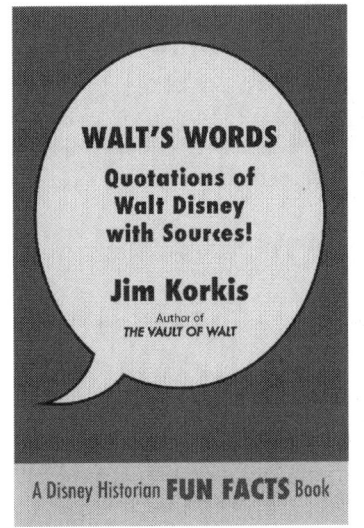

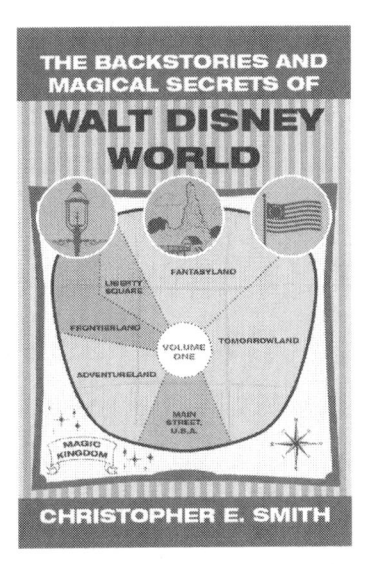

Read more about these books
and our many other titles at:
www.ThemeParkPress.com

Made in the USA
San Bernardino, CA
26 September 2018